The Lost

BOOK of PETER

© 2011 by C E Daffin
www.bookofpeter.com

These are the words and life of Peter, a disciple of Christ, documented by his travel companion Clement, seven years after the resurrection. While not considered part of the official biblical canon today, it clearly answers in detail many questions that modern Christians have been seeking:

Why were we created?
What is our purpose in this life?
What happens when we die?
Why do bad things happen to good people?
Why do some have an easy life, while others suffer?
Who is God? Who is Christ?
Who is the devil and demons?
Where do these unwanted thoughts
in my mind come from?
Why and how was evil created?
Why the Eucharist? Why baptism?
What does "fasting" have to do with anything?
How did the Mayans & Egyptians, and man in general,
acquire all of their technology
and the knowledge of stars and planets?

Dedicated to all the people in the world.

Especially, to my Aunt Dora,
wife Bettye, sons Charles & Blake,
mother Peggy and the Holy Spirit.

Contents   Page

Prelude

Adolf Bernhard Christoph Hilgenfeld a German Protestant theologian in the late 1800's said : "There is scarcely a single writing which is of so great importance for the history of Christianity in its first stage, and which has already given such brilliant disclosures at the hands of the most renowned critics in regard to the earliest history of the Christian Church, as the writings ascribed to the Roman Clement, the Recognitions and Homilies."

I have been asked or pondered questions the Bible does not clearly answer:

What is my reason for existing? Do I have a purpose?
Why does a Good God allow bad things to happen to good people?
Why are some people born "with" and others born "without"?
Why would a Good God create an evil devil?
What exactly happens when you die?

Well, the words of St. Peter explain it clearly..

The Book of Peter is a mixed and paraphrased composition of several nineteen hundred year old documents.

The Recognitions and Homilies of Clement by Philip Schaff 1892
Ante-Nicene Fathers by Rev. Alexander Roberts and James Donaldson. 1873
Acts of Peter & The Apocalypse of Peter by M. R. James 1924
Epistles of Clement, J.B. Lightfoot 1869
King James Bible 1769
American Standard Bible 1901
Apocrypha

The main resources are the Homilies and Recognitions. They tell a first-hand account of the teachings and testimony of Peter, recorded by Clement, who later became Bishop of Rome, ordained by Peter as his replacement.

Pope Clement I, also known as Saint Clement of Rome, would become the true second Pope after Peter. There were other bishops, but at the time Peter was still in command of the church. Thus Clement directly succeeds Peter as head bishop.

This is an incredible story because it bluntly answers so many questions and now everything in the Bible makes complete sense. Before, I had a lot of confusion on biblical issues: Why should I fast? Why should I take communion? What was the problem with eating "unclean animals"? From any Bible authority you ask you get a different answer. In this book, Peter answers many more questions in detail, some of which are very important for man to understand.

This would be a great prerequisite read before studying the Bible. I wish I had read this years ago for background before I started reading the Bible. We all have free choice to believe or not believe; we just need all the information available for making decisions.

This story is about how to make it to the afterlife, the new earth and Kingdom of God, and back to paradise where evil, suffering and afflictions will never exist again.

As Peter will explain, this present world is at war with the new kingdom to come. The prince or king of this world we live in is the devil, and is referred to as the evil prince or evil king. Christ, the Son of God, is the Good Prince or Good King, of the new Kingdom to come. Christ came into the evil kingdom to invite us, slaves and subjects of the evil prince, to become loyal subjects of His Kingdom and abandon our present evil king.

"Many are invited but only a few will come."

Everyone is aware this is an evil world; we just do not understand why nor agree on how to remedy it. All through time man has complained about the evil in this world - wars, corruption, pornography, murder, theft, and it never ever has changed since time began on earth.

Peace, love and harmony are nonexistent in the present evil kingdom, unless one deserts it and joins the army of the Good Prince. Only then will one's heart be at peace and joy until the new kingdom comes.

The Son of God and most all persons who have attempted to invite people to the new kingdom have been imprisoned and/or executed. They are unwelcome in this present kingdom because this kingdom and the new kingdom to come are at war with each other.

".... men are unable to find happiness, preferring the enjoyment which is here rather than the promise which is to come. They know not the great torment their enjoyment in this world brings, and what great delight the promise which is to come brings."
(2 Clement 10:3)

God wants us to enjoy the wonderful pious pleasures He has planned for us in this life. He just insists we restrain from the few evil pleasures, so that we can have a loving relationship with His Son, now and forever.

This is a combination of the referenced documents with portions large and small edited, and parts removed or added. I have used liberties but never tampered with Peter's core message [see example on page 260]. Much of the story is redundant, but this is good because it needs to be read over and over. Just as Matthew, Mark, Luke and John are repetitive, yet different, the same story over and over for our short memories.

The occurrence of this story related by Peter and recorded by Clement took place during and after the crucifixion and resurrection of Christ. Clement recorded his travels with Peter so it would be documented in writing and a written record sent to James, Jesus brother – bishop of Jerusalem. Clement was well educated, from a wealthy family of royal Roman blood. Peter and his brother Andrew were orphans as children and grew up poor and under hard labor.

So here we are in the capital city of the evil kingdom, in the year of our Lord about 37 AD, Rome, nineteen hundred years ago with no electricity, TV, Internet, iPhone, Mall, printing press or air conditioning, auto nor airplane.

"Where all things hideous and shameful from every part of the world find their center and become popular." (Publius Cornelius Tacitus)

The iron-age had come and the wheel invented. They had wagons and swords and good roads, swords to kill their neighbors with and wagons to bring home the plunder.

Yes, this must have been an incredible site that could suck in every pleasure-seeking human: Rome, the center of the world with such an intoxicating atmosphere, like New York City, where torches lit the whole city at night.

All the pleasures good and bad of this present kingdom were in one fabulous capital city. They gorged themselves on food and wine and they attend the Circus for some great blood and guts entertainment, then capped it off at the bath house for sex of any flavor.

Much more exciting and pleasurable than sitting in a cave, watching goats.

"This age and the future are two enemies at war with each other. One promotes adultery, defilement, lust and deceit. The other bids farewell to these and welcomes the new age to come" (2 Clement 6:3).

Introduction

I, Clement, was born in the great city of Rome, and all my youth, was a lover of chastity, unlike all my friends. I was attracted to girls, but my mind was preoccupied, pondering the dilemma of our reason for being. I was constantly asking who I was - where I came from and where I was going. Was there life after death or was this all there was to it? When I die will I ever be again? Did I exist before I was born? Will I remember this life after I die, or will the rolling of time condemn all to nothing but silence with no remembrance that we ever existed?

My mind would ponder over and over, when was this world made? Who made it? Did anything exist before it? If it had been made, then like all things created, will it wear out like our bodies and dissolve back from which it came? Once gone will anything ever be again? Man does not have the answers to my questions.

These thoughts haunted me day and night, I know not why, nor wherefrom. The more I tried to cast these torments from my mind, the more intensely they screamed and my anxiety would rise to a higher level. Thus, I conceded to the battle in my mind and would forever be obsessed until I found the truth and put my mind and soul at peace.

From my early years I visited the schools of the philosophers where I learned nothing. Doctrines were put forward only to be disproved and they achieved knowledge of nothing as ideas were built up and torn down just as quickly. Whenever the immortality of the soul existed I was excited; then it was proved nonexistent and I became frustrated.

I quickly learned truth had nothing to do with anything because truth was whatever you would like it to be at any particular point in time. Truth and false depended on the skill and ability of the person proposing his argument.

The tortures of my soul continued. Did truth even exist?

If this life ends in nothing, why do we bother to continue living? All we do is labor in vain and if we were not kept busy working, we stress over our problems. If after my death I will be no more, why not just end this foolishness now? What benefit will come from staying alive enduring my never ending frustrations?

> *"A generation goes and a generation comes,*
> *All things are wearisome;*
> *The eye is not satisfied with seeing,*
> *Nor is the ear filled with hearing.*
> *There is no remembrance of earlier things;*
> *And also of the later things which will occur,*
> *There will be for them no remembrance*
> *Among those who will come later still"* (Ecclesiastes 1).

But what if some of the philosophers and Greeks are right? They say that if we do not live a pious life, we will be condemned to Tartarus (Hell) and the fire flaming river that flows through the depths of the underworld, described as a river of blood that boils men's souls and is reserved as punishment for those who committed crimes against their fellow men.

Or if I live partly pious will I go to Hades (Purgatory), just above Tartarus (Hell), a holding place to await judgment for the errors I committed in my life time?

Then I would think again; these things are all nonsense, the wild imagination of talented minds. Yet, wouldn't it be best to be safe than sorry? Even if true, I am such a flawed man how could I restrain myself from the pleasures of lust, while uncertain as to the reward of self-control? And what is righteousness anyway? Will I ever get relief from thoughts of this sort.

What then, shall I do? I shall proceed to Egypt, where I can find a magician and pay him to bring me a soul from the infernal regions, so I can converse with it. Then he will summon the dead for me, an apparition appearing in the form of a ghost. Or else, entice a spirit, as the Greeks do, with animal blood for the ghost to drink.

My objective: proof once and for all whether the soul is immortal, not from what it says, but from what I see. For seeing with my eyes I will be convinced of its immortality and nothing will persuade me otherwise.

I expressed this project to a philosopher friend and he counseled me not to venture upon it saying, "Some things should be left unknown. If the ghost should not obey the magician, you will come to realize the soul is mortal and sink deeper into depression knowing there is nothing after death. Some say such enquiries will anger the Divinity and that God will punish those who trouble souls after their release from the body." After hearing this, I was hesitant in my quest.

At the same time a report from the east started spreading throughout Rome and filling the whole known world, proclaiming that there was a certain Person in Judea, an extraordinary Person, who was preaching of a Kingdom of some

God of the Jews and saying that those who keep this God's commandments and His doctrine will be welcomed into some kind of new kingdom.

It was said He performed many mighty works and wonderful signs just by His words. Having power from this God, He made the deaf to hear, the blind to see, the lame to walk. He healed every affliction of men and could even bring the dead back to life. There was nothing He could not do and day by day these rumors increased.

Meetings were being held here in Rome to discuss the wonder of Who this might be and the message He brought to us from this God, His so called Father. Then we heard He was executed for inciting a revolt within the Roman kingdom.

Time passed and a man entered Rome from the Judea region resurrecting the rumors proclaiming: "Hear me, citizens of Rome. The Son of the only true living God came to the regions of Judea promising eternal life to everyone who will believe Him, but only on the condition that such persons will start to live according to the will of God, His Father, who had sent Him. You must change your life from evil things to good, from things of this world that are only temporary to things of the eternal world to come. Acknowledge that there is one God, ruler of Heaven and Earth, in whose righteous sight the unrighteous inhabit this present world. If you change your actions and act according to His commandments, He will give blessings to your present life and prepare a place for you in the new world to come where you will enjoy His unspeakable blessings and rewards."

The man who was proclaiming this message was named Barnabas, who said that he himself was one of the Miracle Worker's students and that he was sent to declare these things to those who wanted to listen. When I heard this I was intrigued and began, along with everyone else, to follow him and to hear more of what he had to say.

He was a very ordinary and somewhat primitive man with an unimpressive dialect. Yet what he said with such simplicity, without any craft of speech, things told to him by his Teacher or witnessed with his own being were mesmerizing. He did not argue or debate with people like the philosophers do, but produced many eye witnesses to the sayings and marvels of which he told.

There were in the crowds those with a high opinion of themselves and they began to laugh and ridicule Barnabas who did not find them worthy of acknowledgement, but his ignoring them made them more obnoxious.

One of these self-proclaimed elite proposed a question to Barnabas: "Why is a fly so formed, very small with six feet and wings yet an elephant, so very large, has only four feet and no wings?"

Barnabas continued uninterrupted. "We have been given the purpose of spreading the words and the wondrous works of Him who has sent us and to confirm the truth of what we speak. It is not our mission to argue since it would serve no purpose and would be a waste of time and words. We are only to proclaim this good news and not argue because there will always be those who will welcome this message and those who will reject it. Therefore

I have been instructed not to trouble those who are not interested in the message I have to give them. It would be a waste of the Word, throwing pearls before swine.

"But we must speak of this news for woe to us if we keep this life-saving seed to ourselves and allow good fertile people, because of ignorance, to be destroyed. Why would I waste time discussing a fly and an elephant while people are ignorant of the Creator and Framer of all that exists?"

The elite were in an uproar and tried to silence and shame Barnabas by crying out that he was a barbarian and a madman. As things were starting to get out of control I, knowing not why, thrust myself right into the middle and my voice blurted out:

"It seems this God he speaks of hides His will from the prideful, arrogant and self-righteous who are unworthy of knowing His existence. When you see men before you who are simple and unpolished in language, yet bring you the gift of truth and salvation, you mock them out of disdain. For only men of your class, skillful and eloquent, are allowed such knowledge, not rustic and barbarous men such as these. Thus you are convicted of not being friends of truth, but followers of boasting and vain speakers. You produce thousands of words not worth one of the words Barnabas speaks. Therefore, a judgment of his God will be your just reward. So continue laughing at this man to your own destruction. By your barking you annoy the ears of those who desire to hear and the minds that are prepared to accept. What a waste of humanity when you self-righteous do violence to the messenger of truth when he might be offering to you the knowledge of the true God. Even if he brought you nothing, you should welcome him and be courteous. Therefore it is you who are the barbarians and he the eloquent."

My words were interrupted as anger was then aroused as much against me as against Barnabas. I grabbed Barnabas by the shoulder and pulled him away and concerned for his safety, I took him to my house where I made him remain.

While we were together for several days he was able to tell me more of this fascinating account. Finally he insisted on leaving in order to be back at Judea for a celebration of his religion. He was also very disturbed at the way the Romans had treated him and would be glad to be rid of this hideous and shameful place.

I suggested that if he were to teach me all that the Son of God had taught him, I could write it down and spread it in a way that my own people would better understand: "Therefore, allow me to travel with you."

He answered: "If indeed you wish to learn those things of which I speak, set sail with me now; or, if you have business, you can come later. I will give you directions to my home."

I went down with him to the harbor and took from him the directions to his home and said I needed to collect some money which was due to me before I headed his way. Barnabas was an excellent guest and had now become a great friend. I bade him farewell and assured him that I would follow shortly. I watched his ship break from the mooring and move down the channel. The crew unfurled the main sail and it promptly expanded against the west sea breeze.

Several months passed while I put my affairs in order and after having collected most of what was owed I set sail for Judea. After fifteen days we landed at Caesarea, the largest city in Palestine. Seeking an inn I learned from people that a Peter, like Barnabas, was also a disciple of Him who had appeared in Judea and Peter also produced divine miracles. I was told Peter would be holding a public debate with a Samaritan named Simon. So I asked directions to where Peter lodged; and having found it, I informed the doorkeeper who I was and why I had come. While I was talking Barnabas came walking out and as soon as he saw me he rushed over and grabbed me and led me in to see Peter. Approaching Peter Barnabas introduced me: "This, O' Peter, is Clement."

Peter's countenance lit up at the mention of my name and having me sit down he said, "That was wonderful the way you received Barnabas, a stranger and preacher of the truth, unconcerned with what others may have thought of you. Therefore the truth herself shall receive you, a wanderer and a stranger and confirm you a citizen of her own city. By giving a small favor, you shall receive great blessings.

"Barnabas has told me everything about you and your dispositions almost daily and without ceasing, recalling your good qualities and how much you are like us. If you are free, come travel with us and hear the word of the truth, which we are going to spread in every place, including again, the lost city of Rome."

I detailed to him my purpose in coming and in my excitement began to ask many questions: "Is the soul mortal or immortal? And if immortal, will it be accountable to a judgment for those things which it does here? And if there truly is a God, what does He require of me? And if the world was created, why was it created? Is it to be dissolved or renovated and made better?" I suddenly stopped myself as Barnabas and Peter were standing there staring at me; "I apologize for my self-indulgence. My soul has longed for the moment of this resolve, so it can finally be in peace."

Peter answered: "Those are the questions for which every soul should yearn. I will briefly relieve your soul, but patience, O' Clement, in time you will learn all that has been hidden from you."

Peter continued, "The will and counsel of God has for many reasons been concealed from men. First, men have only known of the commandments made by men and of their bad instruction. They have entertained wicked associations, evil habits, unprofitable conversation and unrighteous behavior and have partaken in contempt, infidelity, malice, covetousness, vain boasting, and other such evils so much so that the whole house of this world has been filled with an enormous smoke, preventing those who dwell within from seeing its Founder and from knowing what things are pleasing to Him.

"A cry has been heard from the hearts of those trapped inside by Him alone who is not shut up within; a pleading for Him to open the door and let the smoke depart and let the light of the sun shine in.

"He, therefore, whose aid is needed by those in the house filled with the darkness of ignorance and the smoke of vices, is the one whom we call the true Prophet, the Teacher, our Lord, the Prince and King of the new world to come, who alone can enlighten the souls of men so that with their eyes they may plainly see the way of safety through the smoke-filled house. It is impossible to get knowledge of divine and eternal things unless one learns it from the true Prophet because what man thinks of as truth comes from the communication abilities of other men, who are ignorant of the actual truth. This causes what is unjust to be just and what is false to be truth, much confusion with no consensus - the blind leading the blind.

"For this reason piety demanded the presence of the true Prophet, so that He Himself would dispel the false doctrines and re-establish the truth. But first, you must determine the credentials of the prophet himself and when you have once ascertained that he is a prophet, you must believe him in everything and not question the particulars of that which he teaches, but hold the things which he speaks as certain and sacred. He is indeed the Teacher of truth and from no one else can truth be known. We refer to that as 'faith' alone."

Peter then set forth to me openly and clearly who the Prophet was and how He might be found, as though I had Him before my very eyes and could touch Him with my hand. I could feel the truth filling my soul and was struck with intense astonishment at how no one is able to see the answers they seek even when the truth is placed right before them.

Thus, I began to compile a series of scrolls concerning the true Prophet. One set would be kept for us, and the other would be sent to James, relating to him all the teachings of Peter and the actions he performed. For this truth which uttered simply and without craft, derives its power not from show and ornament, but from reality and reason. I am fully convinced that whoever has received this account of the true Prophet can never afterwards so much as doubt its truth and therefore I am confident with respect to this divinely taught doctrine. For every one who hears of the true Prophet will long immediately for the truth itself and will not have to endure the errors of man any longer. How great a gift this was which has been conferred upon me! Be assured I understood its value. So quickly did I get what I had for so long desired that finally peace was upon my soul and I would never let it depart.

Peter said: "I give thanks to our God both for your salvation and for my own peace. For I am greatly delighted to see that you have understood the greatness of the prophetic virtue and because, as you say, not even I myself if I should wish it, should be able to turn you away to another faith. I am very excited that you will continue with us.

"Normally I would never bother to argue with another, but the devil, through Simon, is deceiving many and for their sakes, I cannot just ignore it. So tomorrow I have agreed to a debate with this Simon."

Peter then retired to take food along with his friends, but he ordered me to eat by myself. After the meal, when he had sung praise to his God and given thanks, he rendered to me an account of this proceeding and added: "May the Lord grant for you to be made like us in all things so by receiving baptism, you may be able to meet and eat with us at the same table, as our meal consists of the body of our Lord."

Having thus spoken he ordered me to rest, for by this time both fatigue and the time of day were calling me to sleep.

We are in a battle for our souls. "Good is set against evil, and life against death: so is the godly against the sinner, and the sinner against the godly." (Wisdom Sir 33:14)

Scroll I

Early the next morning a man named Zacchæus came in and said: "Simon puts off the discussion for seven days because he claims he is too busy. However, I believe his stalling will be to our advantage because it gives us more time to study the subjects which will be discussed during the debate."

Peter answered: "Tell Simon to do as he pleases since we can be assured that, Divine Providence granting, he shall always find us ready." After Zacchæus left, Peter said, "He who believes that the world is administered by the providence of the Most High God should not worry himself with the way things happen because in this temporary life the righteousness of God guides to a favorable outcome even those things which seem hurtful or contrary in our lives, and especially for those who worship Him. When life occurrences may seem to be to your harm, you must drive away the grief from your mind because by the government of God, even what seems contrary will be turned to good.

"This delay of the magician Simon has been done by the providence of God for our advantage. In this interval of seven days without distraction, I shall explain to you more about our faith and the teachings according to the true Prophet, Who alone knows the past as it was, the present as it is, and the future as it shall be. Things He told us are not plainly written and that is why, when the Word is read it cannot be understood without an interpreter because the sin which has grown up with men and has blocked out the truth from their minds. Therefore, I shall explain all things to you myself so your mind will fully comprehend and understand."

Peter then began to explain to us, point by point, chapters of the law that started from the beginning of creation to the time at which I arrived here.

Peter addressed me: "Do you remember, Clement, the account I gave you of the eternal age that knows no end?"

I answered: "There always was, there is now, and there ever shall be, that by which the first Will begotten, uncreated, from eternity consists. From the first Will, comes a second Will and after these came the universe and our physical world. From the world and solar system, and their unwavering movements through space, 'time' was created. Then He created the people who loved the Lord their Creator and those people who did not love the Lord. For those who loved the Lord, a peaceful new kingdom of God would be constructed and the rest of the people who did not follow the Will of God were made servants of this present world. God then announced in the presence of all the first angels, why He established two kingdoms. The first kingdom is that of the present time, the one we live in now and this present temporary kingdom is for all the people who do not know or even care to know their Creator. The second kingdom is of a future time, made for those in the first and present kingdom who do love God. And God has appointed 'times', a duration for each kingdom to fulfill. At the end of the first kingdom there will be a day of judgment and on that day, rewards and punishments will be assigned according to the actions performed by all men who ever lived in this present kingdom. The wicked and unbelievers will be consigned to eternal fire for their errors, but those who have lived according to the will of God, the Creator, will receive blessings for their good works. They will shine with the brightest light and will be introduced into the new world and kingdom where they will be given eternal gifts too great to be expressed or described by the words of man." Works will not save one, only faith will, but works will reflect and prove true faith, accumulating great treasures in the new world to come.

Peter said: "Clement, you, have an excellent memory."

Then I continued, "God alone turned the first simple compound into four different elements and by combining them, He made myriads of new compounds that when turned into different and sometimes opposite natures, mingled and created the pleasures of life from the combination of pairs of opposites, first the 'bad' then the 'good'. In like manner, He alone, having created races of angels and spirits by His will, populated the heavens; as also He decked the visible firmament with stars. He assigned the paths of planets and stars and arranged their courses and He completed the earth for the production of fruits. He set bounds to the sea and the dry land and created Hades as a temporary holding place for souls who would die then filled all places on earth with air for life to breathe. In the beginning, when God had made the heaven and the earth, as one house, there were shadows cast by useless bodies involved in darkness, but when the Will of God had introduced light that darkness which had been caused by the shadows of bodies quickly disappeared. Then light was appointed for the day and darkness for the night and there was also water between heaven and earth that became a frost and then a solid crystal type that separates heaven from earth. So the universe was divided into two portions, heaven and earth. The upper portion gives an invisible dwelling place to angels and the lower gives a visible place for man. The earth was then covered with living things so all was prepared, that men who were to dwell in it might have it in their power to use all these things according to man's 'free will', that is, either for good or for evil.

"If the earth didn't rotate, would there be a day? If the moon didn't orbit the earth, would there be a month? If the earth did not circle around the sun, would there be a year? Would time exist without the unchanging predetermined movements of planets and the sun? His stars and planets were placed in the visible heaven to define and give His creation the dimension of 'time'. This 'time' which allows for an indication of things past, present, and future, signs of seasons and of days, seen by all, but are understood only by a few.

"He made a Paradise on Earth, which also He named a place of delights. Then He made man, on whose account He had created this earth and everything on it. All was made and given to man for his enjoyment - a playground for God's children.

"All things therefore being completed which are in heaven, and on earth, and the human race having multiplied, angels came to earth in human bodies to help man keep Gods will. (Genesis 6, Jubilees 4:15, Enoch 6:7)

"They were watchers for God, custodians of the playground, but with time, losing their self-control, they were lured by the beauty of human women and fell into promiscuous and illicit affairs with these human women. Even being of different substance, they were sucked in to the pleasures of man and instead of helping man, they became bad company, acting disorderly and without discretion. This changed the state of human affairs and the divinely prescribed order of life, so that either by persuasion or force these 'fallen angels' compelled all men to sin against God their Creator. In the ninth generation, from the affairs of these angels and women were born giants, angel-human crossbreeds. They were men of immense bodies whose enormous bones are still shown in some places for confirmation.

"Giants, or Nephilim, were the crossbreed offspring of angels and human women and these are the same characters the Greeks teach of in their Mythology and religion. Even our Roman Emperors claim blood line connections, which probably includes my own blood line. Therefore against these, the righteous providence of God brought a flood upon the world so the earth might be baptized and purified from their unrighteous pollution and every place might be turned into a sea by the destruction of the wicked. Yet there was then found one righteous man by the name of Noah who, being delivered in an ark with his three sons and their wives became the re-colonizer of the world after the subsiding of the waters, along with those animals and seeds which he had brought with him.

"For even in the beginning, when arrogant giants were perishing,
the hope of the world took refuge on a raft, (ark)
and guided by Your hand left to the world the
seed of a new generation.
For blessed is the wood (ark & cross) by which righteousness
comes (Wisdom of Solomon)."

"In the twelfth generation, when God had blessed men, and they had begun to multiply again, man received a commandment from God. It said that man should never taste blood, for humans eating blood was also a reason the flood was sent.

"God never wanted man to kill and eat animals. Adam and Eve did not eat animals. Noah would have taken four of every animal, not just two, if he ate meat. Killing and eating animals was initiated by the fallen angels - the Nephilim. It is a bloody demon sacrifice, referred to as eating at the table of demons. God hated this abomination started by the angel-human crossbreeds since God never wanted His animals killed and sacrificed. But since man adopted this detestable habit God gave rules for the priests regarding sacrifices (Leviticus). The only sacrifice God ever wanted was for everyone to treat and love each other as themselves (Hosea 6:6, Psalm 51:16, Jeremiah 6:19-20, Hebrews 10). 'And God said, Behold, I have given you every herb bearing seed, which is upon the face of all the earth and every tree, in the which is the fruit of a tree yielding seed; to you it shall be for meat. And to every beast of the earth, and to every fowl of the air, and to everything that creepeth upon the earth, wherein there is life, I have given every green herb for meat: and it was so' (Genesis 1:29 in the King James Bible – Our new Bibles changed "meat" to "food").

"There was another problem with the Nephilim being a cross between angels and humans, when their bodies died their souls had no place to go. So they re-entered man's body through the food and particularly the meat that man eats and we thus refer to them as 'demons' or 'unclean spirits'.

"In the thirteenth generation, when the second of Noah's three sons had rebelled against his father, God brought the condition of slavery upon his son's descendants. His elder and younger brothers meanwhile lived in the middle region of the world, the country of Judea. The younger obtained the eastern half and the older the western. In the fourteenth generation one of the cursed descendants of the second son became the first human to erect an altar to unclean spirits, for the purpose of magical arts, and offered at the altar animals they killed, bloody sacrifices. So man again, against God's orders, were killing and eating animals and their blood.

"In the fifteenth generation, for the first time, men set up an idol and worshipped it. Until that time the Hebrew language, which had been given by God to men, was their idol, not a hand-made image to represent God.

"In the sixteenth generation the sons of men migrated from the east and coming to the lands that had been assigned to their fathers, each one marked the place of his own territory by his own name.

"In the seventeenth generation Nimrod I reigning in Babylonia, built a city and taught the Persians to worship fire.

"In the eighteenth generation walled cities were built, armies were organized and armed, judges and laws were sanctioned, temples were built and the princes of nations were honored as gods.

"In the nineteenth generation the descendants of Noah's second son who had been cursed after the flood, lusting for more, expanded out of his territory into the western regions violently driving the descendants of the younger and older sons out of their inheritance in Judea and he pursued them as far as Persia. Then the cursed of Noah's second son took over the land and it became known as the land of Canaan.

"In the twentieth generation a son for the first time died before his father on account of an incestuous crime.

"In the twenty-first generation there was a certain wise man of the family of Noah's eldest, blessed son, by the name of Abraham, of the race of those who were expelled from the Judea area by the cursed second son. Abraham was he from whom our Hebrew nation was derived. Again, the whole world was consumed with errors and hideous crimes and it was destined for destruction but never again by water. Abraham, by reason of his friendship with God, who was well pleased with him, obtained from God a promise that the whole world should not equally perish. Abraham being an astrologer was able from the account and order of the stars to recognize the Creator. While all others were in error, Abraham understood that all things were regulated by God's providence. An angel standing by him in a vision, instructed him more fully concerning those things which he was beginning to perceive and showed Abraham also what belonged to his race and posterity and promised him that all the land of Canaan would be restored to him.

"Jesus our Teacher said He was the One who appeared to Abraham when Abraham wanted to learn the causes of things, so Christ disclosed all things which Abraham desired to know. He taught Abraham the knowledge of the Divinity, the origin of the world, and its end. He showed him the immortality of the soul and the manner of life which was pleasing to God. He told him also of the resurrection of the dead, the future judgment, the reward of the good, and the punishment of the evil, all to be regulated by righteous judgment. Having given Abraham all this knowledge, Jesus departed again to the invisible heaven.

" '...all things have been created through Him and for Him. He is before all things.' (Colossians 1:15)

"But before the True Prophet came and Abraham was still in ignorance, two sons were born to him. One was called Ishmael, who sired the barbarian nations and the other Heliesdros, who fathered the Persians.

"He had begotten these two sons during the time while he still lived in ignorance of things. But now, having received the knowledge of God, he asked of the Righteous One if he could have another offspring by Sarah, who was his lawful wife, though she was barren. So she birthed a son whom he named Isaac, from whom Jacob came. Jacob's name was changed to Israel, and through him were born the twelve patriarchs and from these, seventy-two sons were born. When famine hit they all went into Egypt with all their families and for four hundred years, after being multiplied by the blessing and promise of God, they left Egypt because they were being abused by the Egyptians. Therefore the true Prophet Jesus, reappeared to Moses and struck the Egyptians with afflictions until they let the Hebrew people depart and return to their native land. But those Egyptians who survived the plagues were ordered by their king to pursue the Hebrews and when they had overtaken them at the sea shore and sought to destroy and exterminate them all, Moses, pouring out prayer to God, divided the sea into two parts, so that the water was held on the right and on the left as a great wall and the people of God passed through, but the Egyptians who were pursuing them were drowned when the walls of water collapsed.

"After this, Moses, by the command of God, led the people, not by the shortest route which normally took a month, but in circles, for forty years. This was done in order to rid them of the evils they had acquired by living with the Egyptians those four hundred and eighty years. All in all the people had seen Egypt struck with the ten plagues, and the sea parted, manna given to them from heaven that could be made to taste like any food you wanted and drink supplied to them out of the rock that followed them. They were shaded by a cloud in the day-time from the scorching heat, and at night warmed by a pillar of fire. Finally, at Mount Sinai, the commandments were given to them with voices and signs from heaven, written as ten rules, of which the first and greatest was that they should worship God Himself alone and not make to themselves any form, not even any appearance representing heavenly things or God Himself since they had never seen God. But when Moses had gone up to the mount, and was staying there forty days, the people, even though they had witnessed all the miracles of their salvation from Egypt, made a golden calf's head as a representation of God's image, an idol, after the fashion of Apis, whom the Egyptians worshiped. After so many and so great marvels which they had seen, they were unable to cleanse and wash out from themselves the defilements of old habits. On this account, leaving the short road which leads from Egypt to Judea, Moses led them in a circle through the desert, hoping he would be able to shake off the evils of old habits by a new education, but a few weeks' trip became forty years.

"Another of the people's errors was the craving of meat. God did not want bloody animal sacrifices, He just conceded it under certain conditions because it was a detestable carryover from the angel/human crossbreeds. Moses finally realized that the vice of killing animals had been so deeply ingrained into the people from their association with the Egyptians that the root of this evil could not be extracted from them. So he allowed them this one evil for now, knowing it would be corrected by the future Prophet whom God would send as His Son at a later date in time.

"Moses tried to break the people of eating meat when God gave them manna, but the unclean spirits inside of them wanted 'meat' (Numbers 11:4, Isaiah 1:11, Isaiah 66). So God conceded until His Son would come, but God gave them specific instructions on what meat they could eat, telling them not to eat unclean meat, meaning certain meats with an abundance of unclean spirits.

"This rule of food would continue until Christ's body would replace the bloody demon animal sacrifices (Hebrews 10:1). As long as Christ was inside of you (Eucharist), you were protected from the unclean spirits in food. In the new kingdom to come there will be no more killing of animals. The wolf will live in peace with the lamb.

"And the leopard will lie down with the young goat, and the calf and the young lion and the fatling together; and a little boy will lead them. Also the cow and the bear will graze, Their young will lie down together and the lion will eat straw like the ox (Isaiah 11:6)."

"So He appointed a place in which alone it should be lawful for them to sacrifice these animals to God until the fitting time should come. At that time they will learn from the Prophet that God desires mercy and not animal sacrifices.

"In order to impress this upon them, before the coming of the true Prophet Who was to reject at once the sacrifices, God would have these detestable places of sacrifice often plundered by enemies and burnt with fire. Then the people would be carried into captivity among foreign nations and then brought back when they restored themselves to the mercy of God hoping they would learn that a people who offered animal sacrifices would be driven away and delivered up into the hands of the enemy, but they who were merciful and righteous to fellow men and did not kill His animals were freed from captivity and restored to their native land. As usual, very few would ever understand this.

"With this evil habit partially resolved until a later date (the advent of Christ), Moses put Aaron in charge over the people and they proceeded to leave their wanderings and enter the land of their fathers, the land they had before the descendants of Noah's second son drove them out, but before they entered, Moses, by the command of the living God, went up to a certain mountain and there died in secret and to this day only God knows his burial place. As they moved in, retaking their land by the orders of God, the wicked inhabitants were destroyed or driven out.

"Many of the inhabitants were Nephilim, Giants, blood survivors of the flood. So God used His people to selectively purge the land of the remnants. As David was with Goliath, God was brutal with these people, sometimes killing women and children in order to rid the world of their evil influence and Nephilim blood line. God knew the children would be better off raised in heaven's nursery than raised by these demon beasts condemning their own children to eternal Hell (2 Samuel 21:16-22, 1 Chronicles 20:1-8).

"Those Canaanites who occupied the holy land You hatted for their detestable practices, their works of sorcery and unholy rites, their merciless slaughter of children, and their sacrificial feasting on human flesh and blood.....Judging them little by little You gave them a chance to repent, even though You knew their origin (angel –human crossbreed) *was evil and their wickedness inborn,* (in their genes)
and that their way of thinking would never change… for they were an accursed race from the beginning (Wisdom of Solomon)."

"The land was then parceled off by lot. Since God was their King they were ruled by subordinate judges directly accountable to God and for a while the people remained in peace, but they continually desired a human king, another Nephilim, 'watcher', holdover. They also built a temple where they prayed to God, thus instituting another error; a temple was an idol fashioned of human hands. The people couldn't seem to control the desires of those unclean spirits inside of them and by the influence of wicked king after wicked king the people backslid into greater and greater impiety.

"The time began to draw near that the Prophet, Jesus, should appear whom Moses had foretold. The Prophet would warn them by the mercy of God to cease from killing and sacrificing animals, but because the habits of man were so deeply engrained with errors, without animal sacrifice, the people felt they needed to do something physical for remission of sins. Forgiveness could not be as simple as a gift without having to earn it. So, Jesus instituted baptism by water among them in which they might be washed from all their past sins on the invocation of His name, and for the future, 'go and sin no more'. Purification was no longer by the blood of beasts, but by the Wisdom of God, just as the flood was a baptism - a washing, cleansing, and rebirth of a purified new world.

"Everyone believing in the Prophet and being baptized in His name shall be kept unhurt from the destruction of the future war (Armageddon) which will overwhelm the unbelieving world and the suffering it causes will make the unbelieving obey God against their own will. The believers by their 'free will' who chose to love God are now His children and desire to keep their

Father's rules out of love, but those who refused God's invitation, in the end, will have their 'free will' stripped from them.

"So, now in time, we come to the arrival of God's Son, Jesus, The Christ, our Teacher, bringing signs and miracles as His credentials. Even with these signs some of the people would not believe and what was even worse, to their own self destruction, they ridiculed and insulted the Son of God. Adding blasphemy to unbelief, they said that He was a gluttonous man and a belly slave and that He was controlled by a demon. The One who was only good had come for their salvation and by their calling the Holy Spirit an unclean spirit they had dammed themselves with the unforgivable sin. The 'Helper' can be resisted, quenched or grieved but one can never refer to the Spirit as the devil or one of his demons. This can only come from an unbeliever because a believer knows who Christ is and knows who the devil is. It is not what goes into you from the outside it's what comes out of your heart and mouth – your words that condemn you."

Peter broke in: "That Clement is word for word."

Then Peter took over: "Wickedness so strongly prevails in this present world by the agency of the evil prince and his caretakers that Christ assembled an army starting with twelve men, the first who believed in Him, whom He named apostles and afterwards added another seventy-two disciples, so that there would be enough to serve the many people who came to believe in the Prophet. Even though the true Prophet cured every sickness and brought many miracles and preached eternal life, He was rushed by wicked men to be killed and His message buried with Him, but in the end this turned out for the good. While He was suffering, the world suffered with Him. For the sun was darkened, the mountains were torn asunder, the graves were opened, the veil of the temple wall was ripped. Though the world was moved the devil's slaves, the self-righteous, quickly forgot.

"Since God's own Jewish people were stubborn and refused the invitation into the new kingdom, God opened the door to all other people of the world, the gentiles. This had to be done so God could fill the quota of people needed for His Son's new kingdom. When a certain number of saved souls is achieved by all who have ever lived on this earth, the number required to occupy the Kingdom to come, then the time will have arrived. After Armageddon and judgment this present world will be collapsed and rolled up in order to make room for the new earth and kingdom to come. After this world is destroyed by fire, a new world will spring forth and the invisible heavenly kingdom will become visible on earth.

"Therefore the preaching of the blessed kingdom of God is sent throughout the world. On this account worldly unclean spirits are disturbed, the useless bodies involved in darkness, who always oppose those who are in quest of liberty and freedom from the evil prince of this kingdom. They work hard to keep man in error so as to destroy God's wonderful plan for bringing man back into His family. Those who resist these spirits and toil and struggle against them shall attain the desired safety and the victory trophy, the new kingdom.

"For our struggle is not against flesh and blood, but against the rulers, against the authorities, against the powers of this dark world and against the spiritual forces of evil in the heavenly realms" (Ephesians 6:12).

"After Christ had suffered for us and darkness had overwhelmed the world from the sixth even to the ninth hour, the sun came back out and the planets returned to their usual course. Then the same wicked men returned to their former practices, their previous fear forgotten. They guarded the grave with every resource they could muster using their own people, plus Roman guards, who would be burned alive if a prisoner escaped them. Then the incomprehensible happened: Christ's body was gone! They realized punishing the guards would have publicly confessed the true Son of the God of creation to the world, because everyone would know it was impossible for anyone or anything to get past the guards. So they said, 'His disciples took the body', we the disciples? All of us but John were so deeply in hiding, we didn't even know the whereabouts of each other. Fear had us bound and chained, but then the day of His return, words and emotions will never describe - only to live it, only to have been there! We were all filled with a Spirit of strength and peace and it overwhelmed our bodies and our minds, fear fled from us forever, never to return again.

"The truth everywhere prevailed and we disciples, who were very few, in the course of just a few days became so many we were more in number than the enemy forces were. The Jewish priests were in a panic because their lives were all about money. Should all the people come over to our faith, their services would cease to exist and they would have to work like the rest of us. Those scheming vipers would request our presence so we could educate them in our faith and about Jesus, but they had no intention of learning and would postpone every date we set for them to learn of the true Prophet.

"Time has gone by since the passion of our Lord. The Church of the Lord, which we organized in Jerusalem, multiplied and grew rapidly, being governed by the most righteous James, James the Just, the brother of Christ, who was ordained bishop by the Lord Himself. So now here we are today with a great and wonderful task ahead of us: fill the new kingdom quota of souls and earn for yourself great treasures in the new eternal kingdom."

We took a break for some water and olives then Peter began again: "Whenever the soul is distracted concerning some bodily want such as food or thoughts of desires, it does not properly comprehend the instructions that are presented to it. Therefore I delay speaking to those who are greatly grieving through some calamity, or are immoderately angry, or are in the frenzy of love, or are suffering under bodily exhaustion, or are distressed with the cares of life, or are harassed with any other sufferings. For there is a time for all seasons and one must have a clean undisturbed heart fertile for receiving the Word.

"When I do converse, it has to be done repeatedly because of the forgetfulness of man's mind and the distraction of unclean spirits. The wicked demon steals away the words of salvation and snatches them away from his memory, aborting salvation even though man wishes for it. He loses the way by which life is reached through lack of nourishing spiritual food, which is the Word of our Lord. Therefore we must repeat daily what has been spoken and cement it in our hearts - the truth and knowledge of this world and the world to come, so that we may proceed to the friendship of the Creator. As we travel you will hear the same messages over and over.

"God's friendship is secured by living well and by obeying His will, which is the law of all that live. I will unfold these things to you again and again so the truth becomes firmly written upon your heart because men's souls must be strengthened with the Word in anticipation of evil. So that, if at any time any evil comes upon them, the mind being forearmed with the truth, may be able to bear the attack and repel the enemy with the correct knowledge and the strength of the truth. Then by keeping the Word one will receive many blessings, whether it is eternal life or good health and prosperity in this life, but they cannot be possessed without first knowing the truth of things as they are and by first becoming friends with the Christ, the Prophet of the truth.

"Now the Prophet of the truth is He who always knows all things, past as they were, things present as they are, things future as they shall be. He, who is sinless and merciful, is alone entrusted with the declaration of the truth. The deceived have been and always will be those who thought that they had found the truth by themselves. Yet knowing the truth is available only from the Prophet and many desired to know the truth, but have not had the good fortune to learn it from Him and have not found it and have died seeking it. For how can he find the truth who seeks it from the ignorance of men? All he will ever get is the knowledge of mortal man who is condemned to death, destruction and nonexistence.

"All therefore who ever sought the truth, trusting themselves to be able to find it, fell into a snare. This is what both the philosophers of the Greeks and the more intelligent of the barbarians have suffered. For applying themselves to things in the visible world they will never acquire the truth they seek which resides in the unseen world. Where they seek for truth, it does not exist and they are the blind leading the blind, stumbling into every empty hole to find nothing there. Then climbing out and proceeding on, just to fall into another hole, over and over, until it is too late and their time in life has run out. In this world blind men say there is no black or white, no right or wrong and will never learn the truth until they give up their arrogance. This knowledge is given only to humble men by the Prophet, who is the only One who knows what is pleasing to God."

I, Clement, asked: "You have told me that this true prophet is the Christ. Why do you call him Christ?"

Peter replied: "When God made the world, He was Lord over everything, so He appointed chiefs for the different creations: the trees, the mountains, the springs and the rivers and all things which He had made. Thus also He set an archangel as chief over the angels, a spirit over the spirits, a star over the stars, a bird over the birds, a beast over the beasts, a serpent over the serpents, a fish over the fishes and then, a Man over men. This Man over men we call the Christ. The name Christ is the honored word used in heaven, the title for this position, just as Pharaoh is the king of the Egyptians and Caesar is emperor for the Romans. Thus for the Jews a king is called Christ. True, He was more than a man. He was also The Son of God and the beginning of all things. Just as men anoint their human king with oil, Him first God anointed with oil which was taken from the wood of the tree of life and from that anointing He is called Christ. He Himself also according to the appointment of His Father, anoints with similar oil every one of the pious when they come to His kingdom to be refreshed from their labors and difficulties of the previous life on earth and by such anointing they are filled with the Holy Spirit, giving them immortality.

"In the past present life, Aaron the first high priest, was anointed with a composition of chrism which was made similar to that of the spiritual ointment, but not from the tree of life. He was leader of the people and as such, received the first of all produced as tribute from the people. This anointed one became a judge over men yet subordinate to God, the true King of all. Aaron also judged things clean or unclean - clean, being low of demon contamination. If anyone else was anointed with the same ointment he would be either prophet or priest, as gaining virtue from it. Such anointment bestowed much power to man, but nothing compared to that ointment extracted by God from a branch of the tree of life.

"The Prophet, Christ, came humble indeed in His first coming, but He will be glorious in His second coming. He has come and taught and He, the Judge of all, has been judged and slain, but at His second coming He shall come to judge and shall indeed condemn the wicked and will take the pious into a share and association with Himself in His kingdom.

"He first came to this present kingdom as an unwelcomed guest to invite all the righteous ones and those who have been desirous to please Him, to live with Him forever in His kingdom. For these He has prepared unspeakable great things, but the unrighteous and the wicked and those who have despised God and have devoted the first life and their God given time in it to diverse wickedness, will be handed over to the devil for punishment and retribution. But the rest of the story God has not yet revealed; neither angels nor men know. All we need is to have faith knowing God will give to the righteous an eternal possession of fabulous things."

I asked: "What about all the people who have died before His coming?"

Then Peter said: "You compel me, O' Clement, to touch upon things that are unspeakable. I will let you know only what I am allowed to disclose. Christ, who was from the beginning always present with the pious, secretly, through all their generations, particularly with those who waited for Him and to whom He frequently appeared. But it would be a long time before the resurrection of the bodies that had died and were dissolved, so they could come into their new kingdom. So, if one was righteous and pleased God's will, he would live longer on this present earth and then after he died, his soul is taken straight to Paradise where souls are being kept until the kingdom to come. When the righteous die who lived righteously by keeping God's commandments they will go straight to heaven. [see Heaven, Hades and Hell, page 246] But those who believed and tried to do right but were not able completely to fulfill the rule of righteousness and died with some remnants of evil in their flesh not completely paying their debt while alive, will go to Hades, where their souls are kept in good, protected and blessed abodes until the resurrection and judgment day (Catholics refer to this place as Purgatory). Then, after judgment, they will pay what remaining debt they owe and receive an eternal inheritance in the new kingdom, in proportion to their good deeds they accomplished while they were alive on earth. Therefore blessed are all who believed, even those who stumbled yet kept the faith and continued in Christ, for they eventually will come to the new kingdom, escaping the pains of eternal hell. Their bodies shall become incorruptible and will be the first to see God the Father and shall obtain the rank of honor among the first in the presence of God. We now come to those unrighteous, unbelieving, stubborn, ungrateful and rebellious to Gods law, the weeds of the present world, unloving of God or his fellow man. After death, they go straight to hell and are rewarded with an eternity of torment and affliction for their deeds and selfishness in this present short life they were given. So, Clement, this will be sufficient knowledge on that subject for now."

Peter continued: "Now, it is human nature that people want a man-made truth, one that satisfies their pleasure cravings. They only want to learn what is pleasing and fun for men, but the real truth is, we need to do that which is pleasing to the Creator, not that which is pleasant to each individual. For God, loving all people has made the discovery concerning Him available, even to the barbarians and the Greeks.

"men only desire to have their ears tickled, they will accumulate for themselves teachers in accordance to their own desires and will turn away their ears from the truth and will turn aside to myths" (2 Timothy 4)

"Clement, for anyone to know the things pertaining to God, you have to learn them from Him alone, because He alone knows the truth. If you come across anyone else that knows the truth, his knowledge could only have come from Him or His disciples, since it is impossible for man to discover this on his own and this is His doctrine and the true Word. There is one God who created the world and the universe. He is totally righteous and at some point in time, which no man or angel knows, He will judge everyone alive and all that have died who ever lived. Then He will punish and reward people according to their deeds when they lived in this life. This is why it is so important for one to accept Christ's invitation. By just believing in Christ, one's past is erased and it will not be considered at judgment. Only the rest of his life, from that point on, will he be held accountable for. Christ paid all man's debt accumulated before he believed, while he was in ignorance.

"The souls of men are immortal and that is where God's justice is because it is not over when a man dies; it is just beginning. Some people have lived pious righteous lives and yet, have been evilly treated and sometimes violently killed. Then others have been wholly unrighteous and have indulged in luxurious living, yet have died the common death of men after living a comfortable life. To man this appears to be so unfair because man views life as ending at the death of the body, but since God is good and just, He made the soul immortal and it separates from the body at the death of the body. At that time the wicked man goes to hell as his reward for this first life and there he is punished for his sins forever, but the good man, who was punished for his sins while he lived his first life on earth, will be rewarded by exceedingly wonderful things. So evil men are deceived greatly thinking it is over when they die. Oh, what a terrible surprise awaits haters of the truth because they will pay an eternity for the evils they imposed for their short time on earth. This is why we should feel great sorrow and pray for them; these poor blind souls have no idea, until it is too late.

"God, from the beginning made fixed and perfect heaven and earth, day and night, light and fire, sun and moon, life and death. All His creation had no choice but to do exactly as commanded. But man alone and angels, God made self-controlling, having a choice to be either righteous or unrighteous because they were given 'free will'. Man and angels are the only things in God's creation that have this ability: to determine their own destinies. God also placed before man small things first, then great things afterwards, such as this earthly world compared to the eternity world, but the world that we live in now is temporary and the world that will come is eternal. First is ignorance, then knowledge. So also are the prophets, the smallest first then the greatest last. Everything comes in 'pairs'; first the lessor or bad, then comes the greater or good.

"The present world is female as a mother bringing forth the souls of her children and the world to come is male, as a father receiving his children from their mother. Therefore in this world there comes a succession of prophets having knowledge of all men who are sons of the world to come and if pious men had understood this mystery, they would never have gone astray.

"Then, as I said, some men do not know the rule of combination of pairs. Life comes in pairs of bad and good. First comes the 'bad'; then comes the 'good'. So they do not recognize the one who precedes me, Simon. He is a hater of men, yet is received with love. He is an enemy and welcomed as a friend. He is eternal death, but is treated as a savior - believed to be a speaker of truth, yet is a deceiver."

I then asked Peter: "Who is this, Simon - a hater of mankind?"

Peter responded: "I will let you hear it from those who informed me. There is with us a woman, Justa, a Canaanite, whose daughter had a serious disease caused by the unclean spirits and Justa came to our Lord, begging that He would heal her daughter.

But, He told us it is not lawful to heal the gentiles, who are like dogs that eat any meat they find and breed with anything they catch. We can only run the unclean spirits from the 'table of the Hebrews', but she, hearing this, responded: 'Even dogs eat the crumbs that fall from this table and partake of the table of the Hebrews.' For she had actually changed her ways and no longer conducted her life as a Gentile eating all kinds of meat and having all kinds of sex, like the life of a dog. She changed what she was by living like the sons of the kingdom, honoring the commandments of our God. Wherefore, the Teacher granted her request and drove the unclean spirits from her daughter, returning her to health (Matthew 15:27). Had she not repented and changed the direction of her life, from gentile to the rules of God, He would not have healed her daughter.

"She and her daughter, having taken up a manner of life according to God's law were driven out of their home by her husband, whose sentiments and immorality opposed ours. Even though being abandoned by her husband, she remained faithful to her husband and she held steadfast to God's commands and did not take up with another man. She was also a wealthy woman, which certainly helped her situation. She ended up giving her daughter in marriage to a poor man of our faith. So for company, and out of love for her fellow man, she rescued two orphans and she purchased them and adopted them as her own, Aquila and his brother Nicetas. Then she sent them off to get the finest education available which happened to be in the care of a Simon Magus and they became associated with him in all things he did.

"As they became men they befriended Zacchæus, who was one of us. Through Zacchaeus and the influence of the Holy Spirit, they received the Word of truth and repented their association with

Simon and all his errors. When I came to this place, they came to me and joined us, along with their adopted mother, Justa, and have been with us ever since, enjoying instructions in the truth." After Peter had said this, he sent for them, so they could tell me more of this Simon.

First Aquila began to speak: "This Simon is the son of Antonius and Rachel, a Samaritan by race, of the village of Gitthae. He having been educated in the great city of Alexandria, became egotistic, conceited and vain and he believed he was God Himself. He became very powerful in magic and wanted everyone to call him 'The Christ'. He also calls himself 'the standing one,' which means he shall always stand because his body can never be afflicted, causing him to sit. He preaches that God, the creator of the universe, is not supreme, nor will the dead ever rise again. He substitutes the rules of God with his own rules of right and wrong and says that there will be no judgment by God. So through the ignorance of men he spoils the things of the truth.

"The way he came into contact with our faith was by way of a very popular man named John. John was a day Baptist and the first of pairs to our Christ; John the lessor, then Christ, the superior. As our Lord had twelve apostles, the same as the twelve months to circle the sun, John, the forerunner of our Lord, had thirty chief men according to the days in a month. One woman in his circle of thirty was named Helena. Of these thirty, the first and the most esteemed by John was Simon. As John had thirty, one of which was evil, our Teacher had twelve, one of which was Judas.

"But Simon did not become chief after John's death because he was off in Egypt practicing magic. Therefore, Dositheus, desiring the leadership, falsely told the rest that Simon was dead and succeeded to John's position. Simon on returning, when he met with Dositheus did not demand the position, knowing once obtaining the power of that position, Simon could not remove him from it. Therefore Simon pretended friendship and gladly fulfilled the second position. After a few days Simon started backstabbing Dositheus when meeting with the others and Dositheus getting wind of Simon's activities, came in a rage to a meeting and finding Simon, assaulted him, striking him with a rod, but the rod seemed to pass through the body of Simon as if he were not there. Dositheus, becoming bewildered, said to Simon: 'If you are the Standing One I also will honor you.' Then Simon said that he was, so Dositheus conceded the position. A few days later Dositheus himself, while Simon stood, fell down and died. We, to this day, are suspicious that Simon was responsible for Dositheus's death.

"So now, Simon is traveling with before mentioned Helena, stirring up the people. He tells them he brought Helena to earth from heaven, she being a queen of truth and the reason Greeks and barbarians fought. He then proceeds to mix Grecian myths and Homeric Poems with visual magic tricks and so great was the show, we even believed. Yet, we were aware it was all just deception. As long as what he did was just fun entertainment, we enjoyed and participated, but it took an evil turn when he began twisting our faith, employing the worst thing that could be done to men, deceiving them of their salvation and leading them down the path to hell. The more he performed, the more his personality changed into a madman, possessed of the devil himself and we could no longer recognize or associate with our brilliant teacher.

He went so far as to commit murder and acted as though he was proud of his actions and we should be impressed with his abilities. He killed a boy just so he could use the dead body in his magical arts. He claimed he could remove the soul from the body and the boy would die and then he brings the soul back and gives life back to the boy. Simon claims he takes an invisible soul and adds heat. The combination absorbs the surrounding air and becomes water. Then the water turns to blood, then blood to flesh, creating a man made from air instead of earth. He separates and reunites the soul and the body through this despicable ceremony. If we alerted the authorities to his evil deed, he would just make the boy alive again, though only temporary. His magic is impressive to those in ignorance. He is so possessed that he now keeps the boy's body in his bedroom, dressed in purple and hanging by his mirror."

Aquila was becoming disturbed, so his brother Nicetas took over: "God is a witness that we did nothing impious and as long as he did harmless things, it was fun and entertaining, but when Simon claimed his magic shows were the work of God and later killed the boy, we refused his association. He promised us much if we would stay. He promised there would be statues made of us and placed in temples so we would become gods, worshiped by men and girls, by whom we would receive glorious wealth and all the pleasures our hearts could desire.

"The only thing we had to do was become his associates and keep secret his wicked schemes. We refused, but because of our affection and friendship with him since childhood, we urged him to stop this madness: 'Please, O' Simon, fear Him who is really God. Know that you are merely a man and that the time of your life is short. Even though you will get great riches, or even become a king, the few enjoyments of this short life are worth nothing in the new kingdom. All your ill-begotten treasures will only secure your everlasting punishment and you will be severely judged for the deeds you have done.'

"When he heard this he laughed and I responded: 'You, Simon, laugh at good council and your own destruction.'

"Simon said: 'I laugh at your foolish superstitions. Only the insecure primitive unenlightened mind would believe in God and that man is immortal.'

"I replied: 'Simon, you not only deceive others, but you deceive yourself.'

"Simon said: 'You know nothing of what you talk. You saw me separate the soul of a boy from his body but it was not the boy's soul I communicated with, it was that of a demon. Unclean spirits trick you into thinking there is a soul and they feed on the false desires of the heart because the soul of the dead does not exist.'

"'How ridiculous you sound,' I responded: 'If you acknowledge a demon, you confirm there is another world and a God - a world we cannot detect. You even told us the souls confined to Hades (Purgatory) are impossible to conjure because they are safely protected. You also said that the souls of those who commit suicide are not easily permitted to come because they are guarded in Hades. So, Simon, if there is no afterlife, why would an unclean spirit bother to respond when you call?'

"Simon said: 'A magician is their chief. If they do not obey, they will be punished for disobedience. I have been given all authority over them by the devil himself and they must obey their ruler.'

"At saying that, Simon turned to leave. Hesitating, without turning, he muttered: 'You two may leave if you wish, but it would be the most foolish thing you will ever do. If you disclose our conversations to anyone, as you are well aware, I have the power to create a life or end a life instantly.'"

I, Clement asked: "What are his other exceptional abilities? I heard he makes statues walk and that he sets himself on the fire and is not burnt and sometimes he flies and he makes bread of stones, becomes a serpent, transforms himself into a goat, can change his appearance, changing himself into gold, opens locked gates, he melts iron and at his parties he makes images appear. Dishes will move through the air by themselves to serve him and his guests. "

 Peter answered: "You are experiencing contradictory pairs - Simon, the bad of the pairs, whom you see doing wondrous works to astonish and deceive. He has been given power over the unclean spirits with the authority of the devil himself. These wonders do nothing for mankind but excite the demons in men and if a man does unprofitable miracles, he is the agent of wickedness.

"Those then, are useless signs. Making statues walk, rolling himself on burning coals, becoming an animal, flying in the air. How does this profit man? Therefore I have been commissioned as the second of the pairs and through the Holy Spirit, I shall cast out unclean spirits, curing and healing men of their afflictions, just as our Lord did."

As Peter was speaking, Zacchaeus entered saying: "Simon has put us off until tomorrow because today is his Sabbath, which occurs every eleven days."

Peter answered: "Tell Simon anytime he is ready, we will be available." Then Zacchaeus turned and went out.

Peter could sense I was agitated, and asked: "Is anything wrong?" I quickly responded: "That Simon is such an ingrate, why do you let him run all over you? You are so much superior to that worm." Then I caught myself and, embarrassed, apologized for my uncontrollable outburst. "Forgive me for calling Simon a worm."

Peter calmly said: "When you realize your life is controlled by the powerful Creator, you ignore the trials and mishaps of your own life because people cannot say nor do anything to harm you. With God, everything turns out to your own benefit and to their demise. Therefore, Simon's actions are not even his own but are controlled by the devil and the devil is accountable to God. So this has happened for our own advantage. Therefore shake off any annoyance that befalls you, because all will come to some unknown good and anyone offended by another is falling right into the devil's trap. Never ever hold hard feelings toward anyone because a grudge will only destroy the holder from the inside out. It will only hurt the offended, and the offender will never care and most likely never even know he offended. The offended is drinking poison in order to punish the offender and if you refuse to forgive, your Father will not forgive you and your prayers will go unheard.

"This postponement will allow us more time to prepare for our discussion with Simon. I am discovering that he will use our own scripture to prove his doctrine. Over time, the scriptures have been infiltrated with many falsehoods against God and these discrepancies are easily recognizable and dispelled because anything spoken against God is untrue. Simon, as I have learned, intends to speak of those chapters against God that were added to the Scriptures by agents of the evil one. We can never tell the people that some chapters have been added to the Bible or we will confuse those who would not understand. For they do not yet have the power of discerning and might withdraw from the Word altogether. Once the Spirit resides inside you, it becomes clear what is truth and the will of God.

"So, given our divinely allocated delay, I will instruct you concerning the chapters that were added to the Scriptures and this preparation will ward off such distractions by Simon. When impious men look at the scriptures they are only allowed to comprehend things written that are spoken against God because this is actually Gods will. Only when one believes in His Son is he given the ability to discern truth from deception. This keeps the impious and self-righteous blinded, becoming outcasts from His kingdom. God keeps them blinded and in darkness because of their arrogance and unbelief and only reveals the truth to repenting believers."

I, Clement, said: "As I am new to the faith, yet open to believe, tell me what are the falsehoods added to the Scriptures."

Peter answered: "To start, anyone who truly loves the Lord will not be able to take in, or even to hear, the things that are spoken against Him. You will hear from Simon that there are other gods, that the One Great Creator is flawed and makes mistakes; that God is a creator of error. The truth is that the Lord of all, who made heaven and earth and all things, does not share His government with others - so-called gods. Nor does He ever lie or experiment in ignorance or change His mind. His perfect nature is capable only of good, justice, and truth; unchangeable, wise, unending, unrestricted, uncontainable, the One and Only Creator of the universe and of all that ever was and ever will be. God is loving, affectionate, faithful, merciful, and long-suffering. Remember it for the sake of your soul and destiny and run from anything contrary and beware of thinking otherwise of God.

"God's Son, being worthy to be King of the world to come, fights against the devil who, by predestation, has taken this present kingdom by force thanks to man's errors - the result of granting man 'free will' and the thing that exceedingly grieved our Creator was His children, whom He was fighting the battle for were unappreciative and turned against Him and He was assailed, on account of our ignorance of what was befalling the unseen world. Yet, for only God knows why, He still loved us who had turned against Him by assisting the enemy and He wept over the unbelieving, blessing those who slandered Him and prayed for those who hated Him. And not only did He do this as a father, but also taught us, His disciples, to do the like. It is just the forgiving affection of a Father towards his children, hoping to result in eternal peace for those of us who might realize our error before it is too late and come back home.

"This present kingdom was thus taken by force and so, by the will of God the rebellion will be crushed and the present world destroyed, all in due time. Enough time so those of us, the loyal and faithful to our Creator, will abort the rebellion. Our Father, long suffering, holding no resentment, offers any of us who confess our error and humbly ask for forgiveness, a place with Him in a new kingdom; He will be a just judge as to who is worthy.

"We must lose our stubborn, arrogant rebellious nature and regulate our own actions and follow His commandments, speaking well of Him, persuaded that He is alone good and He, at the end of all, shall sit as a just Judge upon every one of those who has attempted what he ought not. But this is enough for now. At another time I will enlighten you on more."

Evening had come upon us. Peter stood up, bid us good night and retired for the evening.

"Therefore we do not lose heart. Though outwardly we are wasting away, yet inwardly we are being renewed day by day. For our small and momentary troubles are achieving for us an eternal glory that far outweighs them all. So we fix our eyes not on what is seen, but on what is unseen. For what is seen is temporary, but what is unseen is eternal" (2 Corinthians).

Scroll II

Peter rising at the crowing of the cock, found us awake with the evening torch still burning. After we all sat down he began to teach. Beginning from the Father, the Son and the Holy Spirit, he briefly explained some more of the mystery and we were astonished why men have forsaken the truth and have turned themselves to error. Peter explained: "It is really easy for people like Simon to deceive with stories against God, because people's minds from their childhood, are accustomed to take in things spoken against God or to deny the judgment of a Supreme Creator because of man's ignorance and the unclean spirit influence upon the mind. They have learned all their lives the knowledge of this world from blind ignorant men headed to destruction and have never heard the truth that is known only in the unseen world." Peter added: "Nothing is more difficult than trying to explain the truth in the presence of a diverse crowd of people because the truth cannot be told to some people since the unclean spirits inside them only want to hear wickedness and treachery. Yet there are also, in a crowd, people who are fertile to the truth. If we present truth to those who do not care to be saved, we injure Christ who told us not to present His Words to swine or dogs that will roll them in the mud of carnal deeds and their barking wears on the presenters of God's word. I will not present the Supreme Divinity to unworthy ears, but in a crowd I am forced to present to both.

"The wicked one loves God as much as the Good One. The devil is jealous of man and has no love for man, and worse, he hates man and wants man wiped from the face of creation. What really disgusts him is how easy we are for him to deceive and ignorance of our Creator is no excuse. He is convinced we are worthless and would even err without his help; he wants mankind destroyed with no chance for redemption, which would have happened if there had not existed one righteous man, Noah. But the Good one, our Teacher, Christ, our Savior, loves us and desires to give man another chance. So He presents us with a remedy - a way the lost can come back into His presence. For Christ desires all to be healed by repentance, but saves only those who come to know God and He does not heal nor bother with those who do not know Him. Justice does not allow giving the good things, which have been prepared for the children of the kingdom, to the undeserving. The undeserving, being those who are like irrational animals, acting like dogs and pigs and are desperately in need of judgment.

"Such is the loving nature of the one and only God who made the world and who created us and who has given us all things. As long as any one is within the limit of piety and does not blaspheme His Holy Spirit, out of pure love, He will bring us to Himself and although we are wretched unworthy sinners, it is His loving forgiving nature to save us. But some will first have to be suitably punished for the deeds of error in this life because God is just and fair to all. Let me state it again. If anyone first denies Him or is guilty of impiety but then repents and believes in Christ and sincerely works on changing his way of life to that of good, loving the Lord, then he is positively destined for the new kingdom to come, but that same person shall indeed be punished for sins committed against God after repentance. He was pardoned of all past sins; his past life is erased from the book of record, but he will be held accountable from that point on, until the end of his life in this present world. Since he finally believed in Him, he will still be saved for the new kingdom, after any post debt has been settled.

"This is a plain indication of God's righteous judgment so that you will be considered worthy of the kingdom of God, for which indeed you are suffering" (2 Thessalonians 1).

On the other hand, those stubborn souls who refused to repent shall be destroyed by the punishment of fire, even though they might have thought they were good. Unbelievers, who have been impious against the one good God, cannot receive paradise. God is just and that would be an injustice to the believers.

"Impiety against Him is to die without acknowledging God and His commandments, or implying there is something besides Him who really is. For He who truly is, is He whose shape the body of man bears for whose sake the heaven and all the stars submit to serve Him.

"Therefore the love of men towards God is sufficient for salvation. They might receive punishment for disobedience, but **if a man or women love God they are saved.** Nothing more is required. To show their love; **'If anyone loves me, he will keep my commandments.'** [see Ten Commandments, page 256]

"If a person says he loves his spouse but commits adultery, breaking a commandment of marriage, yet will admit his error and repent, love will still survive if the spouse is as forgiving as God. But if he says he loves and continues in adultery, the love is dead and non-existent.

"Not everyone who says to Me, 'Lord, Lord,' will enter the kingdom of heaven, but he who does the will of My Father who is

in heaven will enter. Many will say to Me on that day, 'Lord, Lord, did we not prophesy in Your name, and in Your name cast out demons, and in Your name perform many miracles?' And then I will declare to them, 'I never knew you; Depart from Me you who practice lawlessness' (Matthew 7).

"And the wicked one knows this. So it is critical for him to disrupt our love for God by encouraging us to ignore the Lord's commandments and block anyone who might search for God, because just that simple affection will break man's soul free from eternal hell. Therefore he targets the ignorant for destruction, producing many falsehoods and roadblocks using lusts, governments made by man, planets and belief in anything but the Creator.

"Worthy of rejection from the new kingdom is anyone willing to just hear and entertain anything against the monarchy of God. The scriptures are such that any man can produce many testimonies from them in favor of any dogma he would like, of which Simon will be a good example. Simon has formed his own dogma. You might ask: 'What good are the scriptures if we have no confidence in them since whatever man wishes is mixed with God's will?' Dogmas originate for one reason only, man's selfish pursuit of money, sex and power - self before others. The true religion is based on our Creator and how we treat His image, man; how we interact with other people. God's will is to care for others before ourselves, so do not be moved by what the Simons of the world say, but pay attention to their actions and how they live their personal lives.

"Simon, who is going to discuss in public with us has an obsession against the monarchy of God and he will produce many statements from these Scriptures to the effect that there are many gods, one of which made this world and is not equal, but superior to God. But we also can easily show many passages from them that He who made the world alone is God and that there is none other besides Him."

About that time the day was dawning, and someone came in and said: "There is a very large crowd waiting in the courtyard and in the middle of them stands Simon, filling the people's ears with his wicked words of nothing."

So we all withdrew to the courtyard and when we arrived the whole attention of the crowd shifted to Peter.

Simon said: "I laugh at the folly of men who should love Peter instead of me. The affection should be borne to me instead of wasted upon Peter."

I, Clement, thought: "Just what you would expect from the jealous devil, who cannot stand man loving God more than him or God loving man more."

Peter then spoke: "O' silly Simon, those who are your best friends not only do not love you but even hate you, since you are a seducer and lover of yourself. You profess to proclaim the truth and you had many friends who had a desire to learn the truth, but when they saw you doing things contrary to what you would say, they realized you were a deceiver. Yet they could not recognize your evil intentions because there was no one available with the truth to expose your deceptions, but now the truth has arrived and they are despising you. The people are desperate for true understanding. You act by deceptive arts, hoping you will escape detection, but your darkness is now exposed by the light of truth.

You are driven into a corner and being unwilling to listen, you will always be ignorant of the truth. There is nothing hidden which shall not be known, nor covered which shall not be disclosed.

Simon answered: "Let's get to the point. You said that you could show the power of the eternal light and that there are only two heavens, both created. The higher is the home of that light in which the Father dwells alone forever and after heaven was made this visible world was made, where we presently live. You say that this visible evil world is to pass away and a good world will be born. Since your God, as you say, made all things, why did He create evil?"

Peter responded: "The existence of evil is not known or admitted by everyone because only the true Prophet knows of it. Every motion is divided into two parts, one part is moved by necessity, and the other by will. Those by necessity are always in constant predictable motion, but those which are moved by their 'will' can vary. For example, the sun's motion is fixed and predictable and every state and service of heaven depends upon fixed motions. The sun, moon, and earth, are in a fixed unchangeable motion through time and space, but man can vary his state. He can choose or change his direction. Man directs the voluntary motions of his own actions. Thus the things of necessity are unable to do anything else, but men and angels have a power of will, which gives them free choice to do what they desire. Life is where their will leads them. It is where their hearts are and the desires of their minds direct them. This 'free will' creates either 'good' or 'evil', depending on the direction one chooses. Good and evil are contrary pairs that define each other. 'Good' could not exist unless there was 'evil'. Therefore God has arranged rewards to those who do well, and penalties to those who do evil. Neither God nor the devil creates evil; man brings evil into existence by his own actions. Man's and angel's own 'free will' created evil."

Simon responded: "Why didn't a good God just make us all good so we should not have it in our power to be otherwise?"

Peter answered: "As I just said, there is no such thing as 'good' unless there is 'evil'; they both define each other. For if He had made us of an unchangeable nature and incapable of being moved away from good, we would not really be good, because we could not be anything else. It would not be of our choice that we were good and our 'free choice' would be non-existent and what we did would not be of our choosing, but of the necessity of our nature, which brings us to love. How could you love God if there were no other choice? Love does not happen by force. We all wish we could force someone to love us, but that just causes them to hate us because to be true and solid it has to come from their own free choice. Some things God has predestined; the rest is your choice. God does not want forced love because it would be no love at all and it would be against God's nature which is Truth. So in order to have enough people who felt the same for God as He feels for us, the world requires long periods of time, until the number of righteous loving souls which were needed to fill the new kingdom should be completed and then the present visible world will be folded up like a scroll and the heaven that previously was invisible will appear and the souls of the blessed, being restored to their bodies, will be brought forth into light. After judgment in the resurrected old bodies we will be changed into new bodies and will be of such composition that they can enjoy God's light, the glorious light that would have killed the old flawed bodies. But the souls of the wicked, the unloving, for their impure actions, will be plunged into the abyss of unquenchable fire, to endure punishments through eternity."

Simon answered: "If that visible heaven and this earth, is, as you say, to be dissolved, why was it created in the first place?"

Peter answered: "It was made for the sake of this present life of men, a testing ground, a battle training camp and those who pass training go to the new world. This present world and kingdom were created to separate the bad ones from the good worthy ones, the keepers. Only the worthy ones, the pure of heart, will witness the habitation of the celestials and the abode of God Himself, but for this present time, God has destined as a reward to the winners, those wonderful future things He has kept invisible and secret."

Then Simon said: "If the Creator is good and the world is good, how shall He who is good ever destroy that which is good?"

Peter replied: "Our present world is the incubation ground for the birth of a much more wonderful creation. The shell of the egg may seem to have been formed good, yet it is necessary that it be broken and opened, so that the chick, a more wonderful creation, may issue from it. The chick, being the reason for the whole formation of the egg in the first place. So also, it is necessary that this world pass away so the heavenly kingdom may shine forth."

Then Simon answered: "You said that God is visible to no one, but when the earth shall be dissolved and that superior condition of the heavenly kingdom shall shine forth, then those who are pure in heart shall see God. This statement is contrary to the law, for there it is written that God said, 'None shall see my face and live.'"

Then Peter answered: "Simon, your arrogance has truly blinded you. I will tell you once more. To those who do not read the law according to the tradition of Moses my speech appears to be contrary to it. God is presently, by man's God-given senses, seen by the mind, not by the body but by the spirit, not by the flesh. Yet angels, who are spirits see God; and therefore men, as long as they are men in this flesh body, cannot see Him. But after the resurrection of the dead, man in his old body will be judged and rewarded or punished. Then, only the believers who loved the Lord, will have their old bodies made new, like the angels and then they shall be able to see God. Thus my statement is not contrary to the law. Neither is that which our Master said, 'Blessed are they of a pure heart, for they shall see God.' For He showed that a time shall come in which the worthy men shall be made like angels, who before could only see God in the spirit of their minds."

As Peter was speaking, Simon interrupted saying: "The day is late" and without another word, turned and left in his usual annoying way. Then everyone who was afflicted with sicknesses and invaded by unclean spirits, was healed by the prayers of Peter. After which all departed rejoicing, as having accepted the doctrine of the true God and also His mercy. When the crowds had withdrawn and only his attendants remained with him, we sat in chairs, each having our own designated place. The brethren received their food, the Eucharist, as I ate by myself. After which, giving thanks to God, we all went to sleep.

"For I know the plans I have for you," declares the Lord, "plans to prosper you and not to harm you, plans to give you hope and a future" (Jeremiah 29).

Scroll III

The following day Peter, Simon and the crowds reassemble and Peter started the discussion: "The judgment of God hinges on this. Was a man able to do 'good', but did not do it? It is man's responsibility to inquire and seek what is good and to do it when he has found it. For what good is it to know why the world was made? It would only be necessary if we were going to construct a world ourselves. So, for now, it is sufficient for us in order to worship God, only to know that He made the world for our salvation and how He made it is irrelevant. We will not be judged for our ignorance of how the world was made, only the ignorance of the knowledge of its Creator. We will discover that the Creator of the world is the righteous and good God and we should diligently seek His righteousness. Just knowing He is good will not get us salvation. We have to love Him personally and 'do' His will. In this present age, both men good and bad enjoy His goodness, but in the world to come only the good will partake. He shall be righteous at the 'day of judgment' to bestow eternal rewards upon the worthy, from which the unworthy shall be excluded."

Then said Simon: "So, explain to me if the soul is immortal. For why should I bother to be righteous if the soul is mortal?"

Peter answered: "Some men who are blasphemers against God and who spend their whole life in injustice and evil pleasure die comfortably in their own beds and receive an honorable burial. But others, to their dismay, worship God and maintain their lives with all honesty and yet die torturous deaths, or in desolate places, with not even a burial. That is why this life is just a start;

it continues on in immortality because God is just; evenly fair to all. Death seems the worst thing for ignorant man, but the death of this corrupted visible body means nothing in God's grand plan. Therefore a just God will give rewards for piety and punishment for the impious. "

Simon said: "This still troubles me. Many well doers perish miserably and again many evil-doers finish long lives in happiness. Where is the justice in that?"

Then said Peter: "Simon, take your mind off yourself and concentrate; listen to me again, this very thing that disturbs you is obvious proof to him who can see, that there shall be a judgment and life will continue, for some. For since it is certain that God is just, it is obvious that there is another life after this in which everyone receiving according to his deeds, shall prove the justice of God.

"But if, in this present world all men were now receiving according to their deeds, the job would not be finished. Those who know that God is just give indisputable proof that there shall be a judgment and life is not over because life will be just beginning. "

Then Simon said: "Why then am I not persuaded of it?"

Peter: "Because you are blinded by your unbelief. 'Seek first His righteousness and all these things shall be added to you.'"

Then Simon: "Pardon me if I am unwilling to seek righteousness, before I know if the soul is immortal."

Peter said: "Pardon me also. I cannot do other than what the Prophet of truth has instructed me, as that would negate 'faith'. 'Blessed are they who did not see and yet believed.'"

Simon: "That is an excuse for your incompetence. You persuade many to embrace your religion and in this present life, stop from enjoying many self-indulgent pleasures, in hope of future great rewards. In exchange, they lose the enjoyment of things present and are deceived with hopes of things future. For as soon as they die their souls are extinguished, never to be again. 'Eat, drink and be merry, for tomorrow we die.'"

Peter, rubbing his forehead with his hand and shaking his head muttered to himself: "Pearls before swine."

Then Peter responded: "Simon, you old serpent, you have no intention of desiring to ever know the truth because your whole being is to deceive souls. Your goal is to produce many false doctrines that will make you feel good about yourself since the only things on your mind are money and prestige. You are only here to find excuses and acceptance for your behavior, whereby you can satisfy your evil desires without guilt and not worry about judgment or punishment. You strive to suppress God and His commandments so there will be more evil doers like yourself and our loving God will show mercy in the end and not destroy so many, but God is just, perfect, true and incapable of change. Foolish, foolish man you are. God is offering you mercy right now. Something you of all people certainly do not deserve. I pity the souls which you are endeavoring to deceive and devour, but those who are really ignorant of this, I shall fight to rescue from the many you want to take down with you.

"A question for you Simon: 'Which of the two can better persuade a stubborn man, seeing or hearing?'"

Then Simon said: "Seeing."

Then Peter said: "Why then do you wish to learn from me, by words, that the soul continues after the body dies, when you see it with your own eyes?"

Then Simon: "I know not what you speak."

Then Peter said: "If you do not know, go now to your house and go into your bedroom where you will see a murdered boy clothed in purple, hanging by your mirror. Ask him and he will inform you by seeing. For what need is there to hear from him if the soul is immortal, when you see it standing before you? But if you know not what image I speak of, let all of us go with you to your house."

Simon, stunned, changed color and became bloodless. His face became hideous and all of us but Peter backed away in astonishment. When he spoke, his voice was that of another: "I stood by you and spoke with you in my goodness and bore patiently with you, but now you shall see the power of my divinity, so that you shall quickly fall down and worship me. I, Simon, am the first power, who am always and without beginning; not your Christ you worship, but I, myself. Having entered the womb of Rachel, I was born of her as a man that I might be visible to men. I have flown through the air, been mixed with fire and made statues to move. I made lifeless things live and have flown from mountain to mountain upheld by angel hands. I am the Son of God, enduring to eternity and those who believe in me endure forever. But your words are all vain, nor can you perform any real works such as I. Unlike me, your Prophet could not even deliver himself from the suffering of the cross."

Peter answered: "Do not meddle with the things that belong to others. You in fact are a magician, with the power of the devil which is much subordinate to the awesome power of our God, proved by the very deeds that you have done, deeds that are worthless to man. Our Master who is the Son of God, produces 'good' in all He does.

"If you will not confess that you are a magician, let us go with all these people to your house and then it will be evident who is a magician and who is the 'Son of God'."

Then Simon as usual, without another word, turned and left. We all just stood in frozen silence and unbelief of what we had just witnessed.

Peter broke our trance: "You, my brethren, should bear with wicked men patiently, knowing that God could cut them off at any time but prefers to suffer them till the day appointed. Thus we must be as our Lord and suffer them also and resist retaliation for the wrongs they do us. Stand firm against them with the Word of truth but do not let them get to you. If the wicked one had not found Simon to be his minister, he would doubtless have found another. For in this life, those false prophets and ministers of evil must come 'but woe to that man by whom they come'. Instead of anger, have pity and forgive them. They have no idea what they do. If they could only be taken to Hell for just one day, they would abruptly stop their errors. But then, who would attend to Satan's mission? Simon is rather to be mourned over because he has become a choice vessel for the wicked one, possessed by the devil himself, which could have never happened if Simon's former sins had not allowed the demons to walk in the open door of his soul. He is so deluded by powerful unclean spirits, that not even I, but only our Christ Himself could cast them out.

"For there are men to whom, as being perfect in crimes, the wicked one appears, that he may deceive them so that they may never be turned to repentance.

"But those of you with us now, who are turned to the Lord by repentance, bend to Him your knees." When Peter had said this, all the people knelt and bowed. Peter, looking towards heaven, prayed for them that God, for His goodness, would receive those giving themselves to Him and after he had prayed, he instructed them to meet early the next day. Then he dismissed us all. Each accordingly having taken food, we all went to sleep.

"Without faith it is impossible to please God, because anyone who comes to him must believe that he exists and that he rewards those who earnestly seek him" (Ephesians 6).

Scroll IV

Peter, rising at his usual hour of the night, found us waking, so we all took our positions. Then Niceta, was the first to speak: "I have something to ask of you."

Then Peter said: "Ask whatever you please."

"How is this Simon, who is the enemy of God, able to do all these incredible things? He does tell the truth about some of the wonders he does."

Peter answered: "First let me back up and explain again. God, who is one and true, has created you and everything you see for the sole purpose of preparing good and faithful friends for His first begotten Son. That is the sole reason man and everything you see was created - for good companions for His wonderful Son. We the believers, in order to have true fellowship with His Son, have to be good, just as the Father and the Son are good, but man cannot be good unless he receives the Spirit, the Helper, helping us keep His commandments and becoming 'good'. Not by force as the old covenant unsuccessfully attempted, using Moses' laws, but out of love for God from within, thus loving His rules. His commandments are the definition of 'good' and with the Spirit inside of us, our 'free will' will desire 'good'. Foreseeing the result of 'free will' would make some choose good things and others evil, the human race would become divided into two classes and He has permitted each class to choose both a kingdom and a king. The good King rejoices in the 'good' and the wicked king rejoices in the 'evil'- each man's choice.

"First of all he is evil, in the judgment of God, who will not inquire what is best for him. For how can anyone love another, if he does not love himself? Or to whom will that man not be an enemy, who cannot be a friend to himself? In order therefore, that there might be a distinction between those who choose 'good' and those who choose 'evil', God has concealed that which is best for men, which is the possession of the kingdom of heaven. This 'good news' God has laid up and hidden as in a secret place, so that no one can obtain it by his own power or knowledge. Yet He has sent Word of its existence into this evil kingdom through prophets throughout the generations of men, so that lovers of good, hearing it, will hunger and thirst for more knowledge of it, but they must ask for access to it from Him who has hidden it - not from man, not from government, not from astrology, but by praying to the only One who holds the key. Such persons will only be answered if they desire this secret above the desires of this evil kingdom.

"And under no other condition can anyone even understand it, however wise he may seem. Those wise who neglect to inquire what is profitable to them are self-haters and self-enemies and are deprived of its good things, as lovers of evil things. This is why we are bewildered that self-professed wise men like Simon cannot see. They laugh and ridicule our doctrine, yet to the humble man, it is so obvious, but God will not allow the arrogant to know the truth.

"Therefore the searchers of good, through sincere prayer, are filled with the Holy Spirit to love that way above all things - above riches, glory, rest, parents, relatives, friends and everything in this world. He, who perfectly loves this new possession of the kingdom of heaven, will undoubtedly cast away all practice of evil habit, negligence, sloth, malice, anger and such like. For if you prefer any of these to it, as loving the vices of your own lust more than God, you will not gain the possession of the heavenly kingdom. Truly it is foolish to love anything more than God. For whether they be parents they die, or relatives, they do not continue, or friends. Yes how quickly a supposed 'true friend' can change on you. God is the absolute only one you can trust and He alone is eternal and abides unchangeable. He, therefore, who will not seek after that which is profitable to him is evil, to such an extent that his wickedness exceeds the very prince of impiety. He abuses the goodness of God to the purpose of his own wickedness and pleases himself, neglecting the good things of his own salvation and by man's own self destruction, the evil one rejoices.

"So, as I move through the present kingdom, informing people of this treasure, I will always encounter Simons, placed in my path by the evil king to resist me, doing magic assisted by demons. The 'wonders' Simon does do nothing to help man. It is what little power the devil is allowed to use and deceive the ignorant. There is no reason for frustration because I know the Simons will never see the truth and they are just blockers, put in place by the evil king. We have to realize there will always be Simons that never make it to the new kingdom and not be stressed about it; just knock the dirt from our shoes and move on." [see The Creed page 258]

Then Niceta said: "How do people sin who believe Simon, since they see him do such great marvels? He flies through the air, mixes with fire and such? If one believed our Lord for His signs and works of power, why wouldn't you believe Simon?"

Peter replied: "Easy, as I said, Simon does no good works, such as works that are for the glory of God and deeds that help his fellow man and are written in the commandments of God. Those are the true 'good works' and the same rules are written in scripture and were with man before Moses. The capability of doing these works will come only by the divine love of God and love from the Divine.

"I will explain again, which I love to do, and repeat the message in every city we visit. God has appointed for this world certain contrary pairs and he who comes first of the pairs is of evil and he who comes second, of good. So by this is given to every man the opportunity, by 'free will' or 'free choice', to make the right decision, whether he is simple or wise. If he is simple and believes him who comes first, it is then easier by divine knowledge to believe him who comes second. When he believes this second one, he will divinely learn from him not to believe the first, who comes of evil. So the error of the former is corrected by the acceptance of the latter. But if he will not receive the second, because he has believed the first, he will be condemned as unjust. When he believed the first on account of his signs, he will not believe the second, though he brings the 'works' of God. He who is a slave of the evil one pleasures in works that do little if no good for anyone - fly, mix with fire, make statues walk, and so on. What in heaven or on earth are those demonstrations good for? But those works which are of the good One, our Lord, are for the help and salvation of men. He gave sight to the blind and hearing to the deaf, raised up the feeble and the lame, drove away sicknesses and unclean spirits, raised the dead, just as He has ordained me to do. Those works and wonders that are good make for the benefit of men and these good works the wicked one cannot do, except at the end time, the end of this present world.

For then he will be permitted to mix them up: expelling his own demons thus healing man's diseases, going beyond his bounds, being divided against himself and fighting against himself resulting in his own self- destruction. That is why our Lord said that in the last times there shall be such temptation that many of the very elect shall be deceived, confused and disturbed.

"To keep from being deceived continue to obtain knowledge of God's wisdom. One must be constant in hearing His word daily, resulting in a love for Him and praising Him with worthy honor, pouring out hymns and prayers, thinking of Him always. The soul which is filled with the Holy Spirit and love of God can neither look nor meditate upon anything except that which pertains to God, but those who have no affection for Him live in darkness and cannot see light and the Word of God bores them. If they attempt to learn anything of God, they immediately become weary and uninterested and go back to their pleasing habits. It is wearisome and annoying to such persons to hear anything about God, because their minds have received no sweetness of divine love."

While Peter was speaking and the day was dawning one of the disciples of Simon came in and interrupted: "O' Peter, please find forgiveness for me for I have been helping Simon. He ordered me to follow him, but when we came to the sea, he went aboard a boat which happened to be there, first taking from my neck a heavy burden, the body of the boy he killed. When he came out of the boat later on, there was no boy; he had thrown it into the sea. Then he instructed me to come, saying that we were going to Rome, where he would please the people so much they would worship him as a god, gifting him with money, girls and all divine honors. He further said if any time after that I wanted to return, he would send me back loaded with riches. I know not why, but all of a sudden I wanted nothing to do with Simon anymore. I told him my feet were in pain and I would not be able to travel until they healed. Plus, I have a wife and children I could not leave. He became agitated and angry and cursed me. Then he told me how sorry I will be for not going and turning without another word, he set out for Rome."

Peter calmed him and offered him to sit and said: "Simon threw his tools of wickedness into the sea, not out of repentance, but out of fear. Since we have shed light on him, he could have been arrested and executed, thus he has disposed of the evidence."

Then the man stood up and told us more. Even though we were aware of the wicked things Simon had done, we were shocked by things we had never known of.

Peter then spoke: "I, the second of pairs, must follow Simon through the gentile cities and spread the real truth. Before I go, I will leave the people in good hands." Then, looking up to heaven, Peter said: "To You, O God, who made heaven and earth and all things that are in them, we pour out the prayer, that You would comfort those in need as they go through Your error cleansing tribulations. Let them not be upset at Your discipline nor loathe Your reproof, knowing whom You love You correct with affectionate discipline as a father corrects the child in whom he delights. Guard them with the right hand of Your compassion and Zacchæus will need Your help as guardian to them." Peter laid his hands upon Zacchæus, and prayed that he might blamelessly occupy the duty of his bishopric. Then he ordained twelve presbyters and four deacons.

Peter spoke to the others: "Honor the bishop as long as he is pious and has the fear of God because he is representing the place of Christ. Obey him, knowing that whatever honor and whatever injury is done to him, it is felt by Christ and from Christ to God. Listen to him and receive from him the doctrine of our faith. Receive from the presbyters the guidelines of conduct and from the deacons the discipline. Take good care of widows, orphans and the poor; teach the young the Word and sustain one another. Worship God, who created heaven and earth. Believe in Christ, love one another, be compassionate to all, and fulfill charity not only in word, but in act and deed.

"Since I will be here three more months, before I leave, I will baptize those who desire it. Stripped of their former evils, their past being completely erased from the Book, they will receive heavenly and earthly blessings as a reward for doing good for the rest of their future on this present earth, but only if they produce righteous conduct and do not fall back. Let them learn the mysteries of the kingdom of heaven. Attend to frequent fastings, and at the end of these three months they may be baptized on the day of the festival in ever-flowing, living waters, in the name of the Father, Son and Holy Ghost. They, being first anointed with oil sanctified by prayer and consecrated by these things, over time will be given knowledge and the ability to understand holy things. Knowledge no one can see or understand until their minds are released from the control of the evil one by this process."

Peter dismissed the crowd and said to us: "It is our duty to bring some help to the nations which are called to salvation. I must set out in Simon's tracks so that whosoever he tries to subvert, I might immediately rebuke him, but so I do not abandon those who have been recently converted to God, I will remain three months and continue to strengthen them. In the meantime I will send out twelve ahead of me in Simon's tracks. If people are very long infected with Simon's evil doctrine, it will become more difficult to recover them."

Deciding to keep myself, Clement and Niceta and Aquila, Peter told the other twelve to proceed to the gentiles and follow in the footsteps of Simon, then report back to him all of Simon's proceedings. Peter told them: "You will also let the people know I will be following so they can anticipate my coming."

Two days later when the twelve had left, Peter addressed the people which were a larger number than usual saying: "Please do not distress yourselves over my leaving and have faith and refer all things to God. As friends of God, stay in His will and commandments and He will always be with you. Just as you invited me for your salvation, there are now others in need – those whom Simon is deceiving and they are in desperate need of a defender, just as you were. Be constant in hearing the Word daily so that the wicked one and his helpers cannot find weakness and come back in to re-afflict your souls and bodies. See to it that no one stumble and accomplish the will of the wicked one.

"Anyone is welcome to come with us, but by no means may they sadden or burden anyone by departing, such as leaving their parents, who should not to be left, or a faithful wife, children or any other person who is dependent on them."

Peter, teaching day by day the three months passed and when the festival day finally arrived, upwards of ten thousand were baptized.

A letter was received from the brethren who had gone ahead in which were details of the crimes of Simon, how, going from city to city he was deceiving multitudes and everywhere slandering

Peter, so that when Peter should arrive, no one will listen to him. Simon spends all his time obsessed with tearing down Peter instead of spreading his foolish destructive doctrines; he teaches that Peter is a magician, a godless man, injurious, cunning, ignorant and professing impossible things, for Peter claims that the dead shall rise again, which is impossible.

Peter had the letter read to all. Then said: "Obey Zacchaeus; I commend the presbyters and the deacons to the people and the people to them and to the grace of God."

For the whole three months Peter had spent at Caesarea, he used each day instructing the people and then each evening he would explain again to us the day's discourse in private with more detail. Since I had an excellent memory, I could retain everything until I had an opportunity to document his sayings and our travels, writing them on the papyrus scrolls. This time I made three copies, one to leave with the local church, one sent to James our Christ's brother who was instructing the church in Jerusalem and a third copy we would retain for ourselves.

As the sun had set, we finished the day as usual and retired.

"Only be strong and very courageous, being careful to do according to all the law that Moses my servant commanded you. Do not turn from it to the right hand or to the left, that you may have good success wherever you go. This Book of the Law shall not depart from your mouth, but you shall meditate on it day and night, so that you may be careful to do according to all that is written in it. For then you will make your way prosperous, and then you will have good success". (Joshua 1)

Scroll V

The next day, I Clement, found the rest of our group awake, but I did not see Appion and asked if anyone knew his whereabouts and someone said that he had been unwell ever since the other evening. So when I said that we should go check on him, someone enquired of my relationship to Appion, so I proceeded to tell a story:

"I remember a trick that I played upon Appion in Rome and he was not of good humor about it. From my boyhood I was always a lover of truth and a seeker of the truth of life and I would spend my time in raising and refuting theories, just as the philosophers did. My family was wealthy and a member of the Roman elite so I received the best education and was privileged to do whatever I wanted and I became obsessed in my quest for truth. Who is man, why we are here and where we are headed, if anywhere? I liked girls but unlike my promiscuous friends and associates, I was a lover of chastity and my obsession for the meaning of life replaced girls and became like an obsession over a lover. Finally, over-stressed, I became depressed and did not even want to get out of bed. Appion was a friend of my father and happened to be visiting Rome where he stayed with us and hearing that I was in bed, he came in to check on me. He was familiar with medicine and felt he might be of some help so Appion asked how I was doing and what had me bed-ridden. Appion seemed to be a very good man and quite intelligent, but he had one irrational issue that really disturbed me. The man exceedingly hated the Jews and had written many scrolls against them and he even formed a friendship with this Simon, not through desire of learning, but because he knew that Simon was a Samaritan and also a hater of the Jews.

"At that time of my obsession with life, there was only one girl that I really liked, but she never knew how I felt, since I did not have the time to waste on feelings. She was brilliant and a lover of philosophy. Well, I was not about to tell him my true problem, for he would just laugh at me and tell everyone else. So I told him; I was suffering and distressed because of a girl and was ashamed to speak of love which, as I said, was partially true.

"Appion replied: 'There is nothing in life which does not ask of help. I myself, when I was young, being in love with a most accomplished woman was crushed knowing I could never have her, but at that same time I befriended a certain Egyptian who was exceedingly well practiced in magic. Having become great friends, I told him of my love problem and not only did he assist me in all that I wished, but he taught me a spell by means of which I could obtain her and as soon as I had her, I would be cured of love. Therefore within seven days I shall put you fully in possession of your girl.'

"When I heard this I said: 'Mr Appion, I no longer believe in magic because I have tried several magicians and they all took my money and produced nothing. Their potions are worthless, but I am still open for anything that would help. They say unclean spirits are direct subjects of human magicians and that they must obey anything commanded of them, so why didn't it work for me?'

"Then Appion said: 'I know a lot more about these things than you do. The demons, by order of the devil, must obey magicians in whatever the magician commands them. Magicians are masters over demons, just as a solider cannot disobey his centurion, neither can a centurion disobey the army general and the army general follows the commands of the Emperor and Senate. So it is impossible for the unclean spirits not to serve the devil who is their commander. When they are called by him, they yield trembling, well knowing that if they disobey they shall be fully punished. So the fallen angels themselves, being summoned by the magicians in the name of their ruler, Satan, obey because if they were disobedient, they would be destroyed. Unless all things that are living and rational feared vengeance from the ruler, chaos would ensue, order would be lost and all would be revolting against one another. So a magician, enchanter and wizard being human, has received the secret knowledge of power over the unseen evil creatures of this present world but not the evil prince himself. The prince only allows the use of his subjects if it glorifies himself; the same for the magician who has been given the correct code process, different from ours yet similar, through potions, enchantments and proper ceremonies to summons the solders of the evil prince for personal use, but only if such personal use has an evil outcome. The granted request may be a deception, appearing good, as in the satisfied love you would get from a mistress, but the end result only satisfies the will of the devil, as in adultery and the emotional destruction of lives. A magician's request must have an evil outcome and will be denied if its purpose was love and the benefit of mankind.'

"Then I said: 'Is it true, as the poets and philosophers say, that for magic to exist there have to be unclean spirits and a hell - a hell where souls are punished for living impious lives?' Appion said: 'That is correct.' I asked: 'What if, instead of using magic to force her into adultery, we persuade her with words and receive her permission?'

"Then Appion said: 'Do you not see it is the same thing by any means you use to achieve it? The result is still the will of the devil whether by magic or by deception. Do you not think it is the same thing whether you obtain her by magic or by deceiving her with words?' Then I said: 'Not really. I can see where to force an unwilling woman by magic would subject me to the most terrible punishment, as having plotted against a chaste woman, but if I persuade her with words she has "free will" and it allows the action by her choice, not force. I had rather die than force her against her will.' Appion said: 'As I said, both are the same. The end result is the will of the devil and the destruction of mankind. It is the end result of every action that will be judged, not the means by which it was achieved.'

"I said: 'She is married and as all others I am sure she has many lovers, but I still prefer to win her over by persuasion and not by the force of magic because she is not only beautiful but very intelligent and a philosopher and will not fall prey to flattery.'

"Then Appion said: 'You underestimate my abilities. We will set an appointment with her.' 'That,' I said, 'is impossible.' Appion asked if it were possible to send a letter to her. Then I said: 'That indeed may be done.' Appion cheerfully responded: 'Tonight I shall write a letter that praises her highly and tomorrow I will give it to you and you can forward it to your new lover-to-be.'

"So Appion did as he said and I, actually, still have the letter and keep it with me." I showed the paper to those who were present, and read it to them.

"'At the bidding of Love, Eros the first-born of all, greetings: I know you are devoted to philosophy and you minister to noble people. My issue is with Eros, for he was created for the increase of people and Eros is the eldest of all the gods. For without Eros there can be no attraction of men and women therefore we are all instruments of his. So my feelings are not of my own choosing since Eros, by means of us, is the fabricator of all that is begotten and he is the mind inhabiting our lustful souls. It is not when we ourselves wish love, but when we are ordered by him to fall in love, that we desire to do his will. But if, while we desire according to his will, we attempt to restrain the desire for the sake of what is called chastity, we would do the greatest impiety, opposing the oldest of all gods and men? According his will and desire I have been struck by his arrow, burying into the deepest depths of my heart, just from my gaze upon your countenance. It entered my eyes as I graced your beauty and penetrated to my heart inflaming my mind and soul. I have struggled relentlessly to remove it, but have finally conceded and I am forever in love, overwhelmed with desire and longing. Now I am hopelessly a slave of your beauty, my heart captured and bound and I beseech you to quench my dying thirst for lust. If you find it not in your heart or your passionate nature then I beseech your elegance to please have mercy on my heart and by your grace, remove this embedded arrow and release me from this wonderful prison of your glowing beauty so I can once more live free again'

"I received the letter from Appion and acted as though I were really going to send it to a beloved one. I, myself, concocted a written response to it, and a week later I gave him the reply, as if from her, as follows:

"'Dear Obsessed; I wonder how, when you commend me for wisdom, you write to me as if I were a beautiful fool. For, wishing to persuade me to your passion, you make use of examples from the mythologies of the gods that Eros was the eldest of all and above all gods and men. So not fearing blasphemy against the gods, you think you might corrupt my soul and insult my body. For Eros is not the leader of the gods, he is the leader of lusts and he lusts for copulation, invading our souls through the members of our bodies, but it is the lustful passion of the lover himself, which is increased by hope and diminished by despair.

"'Your Eros is my Cupid. Even though Cupid's mother, Venus, was adulterous with gods and mortals, she is my goddess of chastity. And the angel Cupid, pricked by his own arrow, descended down from heaven falling in love with the mortal Psyche and so is your issue with desires resulting from your own mishap.

"'Eros is not a god as I conceive him, but a desire occurring from man in order to perpetuate life, so that men will be attracted to women and desire to mate with them. Therefore the whole race may not fail, but by reason of lust and pleasure, offspring may be produced out of the substance of parents who shall die and such offspring may sustain their own parents in their old age. But those born from adultery do not have the nature of affection towards those who have begotten them and will abandon and disown the couple that birthed them.

"'I am not a participant of adultery and believe parents should provide for the chastity of their children, anticipating such desire by education and instruction, so they would not concede to wicked pleasures, encouraging all to satisfy this desire by marriage and commitment to just one and only one, persuading them not to desire any other.

"'I have learned from a certain Jew both to understand and to do the things that are pleasing to God and not to be entrapped into adultery by your distracting fables. I pray that may God help you with your evil desires and impose efforts to be chaste upon your misled mind.

"'As for your soul burning with lust, good luck with that barb of erotic madness.'

"When Appion heard my substituted letter he said: 'Is it without reason that I hate the Jews? Here now some Jew has fallen in with her and has converted her to his religion and persuaded her to chastity and it is henceforth impossible that she ever have intercourse with another man. These Jews ruin it for all of us, damn their commandments. Setting God before them as the universal inspector of actions, they love chastity, believing their God is always watching and will punish those who do not keep His rules.'

"Appion feeling rejected I confessed, laughing, saying: 'Appion, I made this all up. I never contacted this girl because my soul is obsessed with other desires. I made it up and wrote her letter of response. So you have not been rejected. It was all out of fun.'

"Appion un humored left without another word. This will be my first meeting with him since that awkward moment."

The others having heard my story could not wait to see Appion's disposition when we met for the second time.

When we arrived, we found him bathed and sitting at a table furnished. He was very polite and held no hard feelings and was very interested in conversing with us concerning the Greek gods. We agreed on a time tomorrow and bid good night. Then we departed each to our own room.

"No temptation has overtaken you except what is common to us all. And God is faithful; he will not let you be tempted beyond what you can bear. But when you are tempted, he will also provide a way out so that you can endure it" (1 Corinthians 10).

Scroll VI

On the next day, when I came with my friends to the appointed place in Tyre, I found Appion sitting between Anubion and Athenodorus, and waiting for us, along with many other learned men. I greeted them and sat down opposite Appion and in a little he began to speak:

"So let me start by explaining about the gods. The wisest of the ancients who learned the truth, kept this knowledge from all who were unworthy and had no desire for knowing divine things.. ...."

For the next hour or more, we all discussed the ancient Greeks and their gods, heroes of mythology - the disgusting actions of gods and how they came about and were ancestors to the Nephilim. The Greek gods started with the "watchers", angels sent from heaven to Earth to get man back in line with God. The leader of the "watchers" was Zeus, the devil himself, the "God wannabe", but it seems women's beauty can even overpower angels. They began to lust after human women and chose to defect and live among men. They produced children by human women and the offspring of these affairs were known as the Nephilim. The Nephilim were savage giants who pillaged the earth and endangered humanity and God's plan for man. They taught humans to make metal weapons, cosmetics and other necessities of civilization that had been kept secret in heaven. They also introduced man to meat eating, killing God's animals. This led to killing other people for food, later to be known as "The bloody demon sacrifice." Most were annihilated by a great flood because these so-called gods murder their children and have incestuous affairs of all kinds, shameless adulteries and countless impurities and persuaded man to do the same.

Then we talked of creation and how the poets now say nature was the first cause of the whole creation and the first moving and mixture came from the earth and there is no God.

Yet, even when they assert that it was nature which fashioned the universe they were unable to clearly demonstrate this on account of the traces of design in the work. So they used words with no proof to bring in organization and direction of order, like that of the foresight of mind, in such a way that they were able to entrap even the wisest, but we say to them: "If the world arose from self-moved nature, how did it ever take proportion and shape, which cannot come but from a creative wisdom and can be comprehended only by knowledge? Knowledge alone gives direction to such things. If, on the other hand, it is by wisdom that all things subsist and maintain order, how can it be that those things arose from self-moved chance? If there was a beginning, where did a beginning come from and a beginning of what?" They claim the "self" in "self-moved" was originally "nothing". Therefore, nothing created everything and then everything arranged itself into complex orders with detailed forms and complicated functions and direction, all by random chance. The whole fabric of our universe came by chance accidents and random combinations. Future man will certainly be humored at how ignorant and silly we primitive men were. How these brilliant minds embarrass mankind! Our Creator stands before us every day in His creation. We see Him with our eyes and deny He ever existed.

"For all men who were ignorant of God were foolish by nature;
and they were unable from the good things that
are seen to know him who exists,
nor did they recognize the craftsman while
paying heed to his works; (Wisdom of Solomon)."

While we were talking to Appion and his companions, Peter drew near and the people were flocking together, hurrying to meet him. So we moved on to greet Peter and Peter enquired as to our conversations and I filled him in. Then Peter told us of Simon's slanders and the monstrous shapes he had taken; then he killed a bull and all ate the meat, a sacrificial feast, infesting diseases and sickness on all that ate and now most of the sick are in need of help. Others of the sick moved on with Simon to Sidon, hoping to be cured by him, but Peter had heard that none of them had been cured by Simon, who had infected them with the unclean spirits through meat in the first place.

Peter had us gather so he could tell us again some of the things the Teacher had told him: "Christ, who has sent us, came because all of the world had fallen into wickedness and man had set the knowledge of truth in opposition of errors, errors caused by man's ignorance of God's will. Realizing many men desired good and would welcome the light of truth, once they discovered they had been deceived, they would repent and become angry against ignorance and the deceivers. Therefore there is a battle which is to be fought by us in this life. **Disclose the word of truth and knowledge to all men and conquer the errors of ignorance**. As we have all seen dead flesh cut away from the living, so the body will live and not be infected by the gangrene. The same is the cutting edge of the knowledge of truth. He who has sent us said again, 'I am not come to send peace on earth, but a sword.' For the sake of salvation, a son or daughter who has received the word of truth must be separated from his unbelieving parents; or father from son, mother from daughter. If they remained with them living in error, they would themselves perish with them. If they convert them and stop the sinful living, that is fine, but he who will be saved must be separated from him who will not. Ignorance and truth refuse to cohabit with each other, just as good cannot have fellowship with evil. Those who receive the knowledge of the truth, because it is full of goodness, desire to share it with everyone, even with those who hate and persecute them, because they know that ignorance is the cause of their errors. If we are taught to pray for our murderers and persecutors, how much more should we pray for parents and relatives.

"We love our parents because they seem to be the creators of our life. This is not so because we were created by God, THROUGH our parents, into this present world and our parents are not authors of our life, but means of it. For they do not bestow life, but afford the means of our entering into this life while the one and sole creator of life is God. He knew us before we were even conceived!

"We can conclude that all evil springs from ignorance and ignorance herself, the mother of all evils, is sprung from carelessness and inattention and is fed and grows in the minds of men because they know not what is going on. Others do not want to know and close their eyes and ears and they fear what learning the truth might reveal to them. Their crimes are negligence, apathy and reluctance to diligently search for the truth. If anyone, like us, teaches that ignorance is to be conquered, it is with difficulty rooted out and therefore all we can do is to make available to everyone the knowledge of the truth. Some will accept and others reject as this was meant to be. The Teacher said: 'Not all will enter the kingdom,' and we should not frustrate ourselves thinking we can override God's will for 'free choice', and force the destiny of man ourselves. What our Lord said will come to pass and you will be wasting your time and energy trying to change the mind of them for whom it will never be. Just allow them access to the word and leave it at that and if they knock on the door and inquire for more, then continue on with them for as long as they are interested.

"You can only lead a horse to water. From there on, it has 'free will'. With the old covenant, they attempted to keep the Ten Commandments by using the 'law of Moses' and under the law they would have beat the horse and shoved its head into the water - forcing the horse to drink, against its free will. With the new covenant, belief in the Prophet by faith alone allows His Spirit to come inside of you. Now a person desires to keep the Father's commandments, just out of love and appreciation. With God's Spirit inside of a person he becomes constantly thirsty for the Word and will happily drink. The old covenant worked by force from the outside in, but the new covenant, once it is securely inside, works from the heart out. With the new covenant the 'laws of Moses' are no longer necessary for man to keep the commandments because man will keep the commandments from love and desire within. [see Old and new covenant, page 243]

"Ignorance is a great evil, but because it has no substance, it is easily dispelled by those who want to rid themselves of it. Ignorance is nothing more than the 'lack of' knowing what is good for us and once we know what is good for us, ignorance perishes. Therefore, one would think, the knowledge of truth would be eagerly sought after and the only one who can give the truth, is none other than the true Prophet - our Lord, Savior and King to come. Through our Lord is the gate of life to those who will enter and the road of good works to those going to the city of salvation.

"Before anyone ever hears what is good for him, he is unaware that he does not know what is in his best interest. What he has learned all his life was from human teachers, so he is unaware of the truth and his teachers are blindly wandering in the dark, stumbling in all directions without the light of truth to lead them to the right path. Forces of the unseen world, which are undetectable by any of mans created senses, are thus easily able to steer man in any direction they choose because man has no idea who is putting those thoughts and suggestions in his mind. But God has also placed in man a desire, a yearning to know God and His truth. Even after all those years of being trained and led around by those forces of evil, there is still a yearning deep inside, but when man is finally presented with the knowledge of the truth, those forces, the slave masters of this present kingdom who have owned man for so long a time are easily able to convince him to reject the truth. At that point man is no longer ignorant and if he continues on in those errors, he will be held accountable at judgment and will suffer punishment, because he rejected the truth and did not spend the rest of his life living well. However, if after hearing, he willingly receives them and is thankful that the teaching of good things has been brought to him and does not cease to learn, giving thanks to God, pursuing a life of good, loving and following his newly found treasure, the commandments of his Creator, he will assuredly receive a reward prepared for him in the world to come. From then on, he also will be astonished at the errors of other men and that no one can see the truth which is placed before his eyes and how silly and ridiculous man's beliefs and truths are. The same man made truths that held him bondage before his eyes were opened. Yet one must realize humans are never allowed to see and understand, no matter how intelligent they think they are, until they first believe in Christ, the Son of God, Creator of the universe and our entire existence. God has put a supernatural block on the stubborn self-important unbelieving, but the humble believer, in the privacy of his heart, continues rejoicing and giving thanks for his newly found treasures and wisdom, delighting in the practice of good works and fantasizing about his future inheritance, the new world to come, when he will meet God, the king and Creator of all.

"While I teach the things which pertain to salvation, if any one refuses to receive them and strives to resist them with a mind occupied by evil feelings and opinions, he has chosen his own path to destruction. It is his duty to examine what we say and compare it to the way he has been living and if he is open minded and humbles himself, he will eventually realize, by the grace of God, that we speak the words of truth. Then desiring to direct his life in good actions, resisting the evil desires of the flesh, he becomes a good possession of the Ruler of all.

"Again, as I have said, God instituted two kingdoms and has given to each man the power, the free will, of becoming a servant of the kingdom of his choosing. And since it is decreed by God, no one man can be a servant of both kingdoms, with all earnestness and with the best of your ability and the help of the Holy Spirit, keep and obey the Commandments of the good King. No one can serve two masters as one cannot serve God and be a slave to the errors of the present kingdom.

"When you have come to the Father you learn that you are to be born anew by means of waters, water being the first created. For he who is regenerated by water, having filled up the measure of good works, is made heir of Him by whom he has been regenerated in incorruption. So come to the Father that your previous errors may be washed away and shown to the Father that ignorance was their sole cause. Now God has ordered everyone who worships Him to be sealed by baptism, but if you refuse and obey your own will rather than God's, you are doubtless contrary and hostile to His will.

"What does the baptism of water contribute towards the worship of God? In the first place, do it because your Father said so. It pleases Him and to please Him is all we need to know. Secondly, when you are born again of water and of God, your former birth you had through man is cut off so that you can now obtain salvation, otherwise it is impossible. Unless a man is born again of water, he shall not enter into the kingdom of heaven. Therefore make haste, for there is in these waters a certain power of mercy which was borne upon them at the beginning, and acknowledges those who are baptized under the name of the threefold sacrament, the Father, the Son and the Holy Spirit and rescues them from future punishments, presenting as a gift to God the souls who are consecrated by baptism. Hurry yourselves to these waters, for they alone can drown the violence of the future fire. For him who delays to approach them, it is evident that the idol of unbelief remains in him. For whether he be righteous or unrighteous, baptism is necessary for him in every respect, that perfection may be accomplished in him and he may be born again to God. For the unrighteous, a pardon may be given him of the sins which he has committed in ignorance. Therefore all should hasten to be born again to God without delay, because the end of every one's life is uncertain.

"But when you have been regenerated by flowing water, living water, show by good works the likeness in you of that Father who has begotten you. Now that you know God, honor Him as a father and live according to His will, His Commandments, His Rules. By loving God and caring for other people. How embarrassing, if at judgment, the unbelieving have done equal or better works than we, the believers."

When he had said these things he dismissed the people, for Peter had now taught the word of God for three whole months, converting multitudes to the faith. He thus ordered me to fast and after my fasting, he baptized me in the constant flowing water of the creeks which flow into the sea. Now I was allowed to have dinner (Eucharist) with Peter and the others, after which, we went to sleep.

"Know therefore that the Lord your God is God, the faithful God who keeps covenant and steadfast love with those who love him and keep his commandments, to a thousand generations" (Deuteronomy 7).

Scroll VII

After a lengthy stay in Tripoli, we left the next day and made our first stop at Ortosias, where we remained there the next day. Many believers had come along and were following Peter. So Peter stopped and addressed them saying: "We need to draw as little attention as possible so let half of us enter the city first, then the rest will enter."

Our plan was to enter the big cities one by one, remaining three months in each. The first group would enter each city followed a day, or more, later by the second group and I was allowed to stay in the second group with Peter. He told the first group: "Friends like us are always together, joined by memory, while we are apart. Just as many persons are near to one another in body, but are separate in mind."

I told Peter that I was glad he chose me to stay with him because he had become the earthly father I lost when I was in my teens - the father I never really knew: "You are the cause of my salvation and knowledge of the truth and I confess, my youthful age is subject to the snares of lusts and I am afraid to be without you. I trust, by the mercy of God, that my mind being trained from your instruction, will be unable to receive anything else into its thoughts and since I am free from a wife and family, I hope you will allow me to be your servant."

Then Peter broke out laughing and replied: "So, Clement, as truly my servant, you will clean my house, make my bed and arrange my beautiful coverlets; guard and safe-keep my rings and expensive jewelry; prepare my robes, which I would be constantly changing; supervise my cooks, butlers and farm hands and provide various and choice meats to be prepared and all those things pleasing for men of my high standing, like satisfying all the pleasures and appetite of some enormous beast. O' Clement, you have been living with me all this time, so you know my manner of life. I live on bread alone with olives and sometimes herbs, as I avoid demon-contaminated meat. My dress is what you see, a tunic with a pallium, (neck scarf) and having these I require nothing more of this world. This is plenty sufficient for me because my mind does not desire temporal things present, but things eternal and therefore no present and visible thing delights me, but I do appreciate your kind intentioned gesture and the offer to give up so much. You are wealthy and have been accustomed to so great abundance, yet have been able so soon to abandon it and to accommodate yourself to this life of ours, which makes use of necessary things alone. I and my brother Andrew have grown up from our childhood not only orphans, but also extremely poor and through necessity have become used to hard labor. Therefore I am the one who will be servant to you."

When I heard this my heart ached, because so great a man, who is worth more than the whole world, would serve me - a man chosen by the Most High God to save the souls of men. Then Peter continued: "Our Lord and King who came for the salvation of the whole world and who was nobler than any creature submitted to be a servant that He might persuade us not to be ashamed to perform the ministry of servants to our brethren."

Then Peter asked: "Is there no one of your family surviving?"

I answered: "I am it. There are many powerful men coming of the blood line of Caesar. Caesar himself gave a wife to my father, a girl who was a relative of Caesar's and she had been educated along with him. My mother was of a very noble family and by her my father had twin sons, born before me. They did not look like one another, as I barely remember my father telling me. I hardly knew them and can barely remember my mother but I cherish the remembrance of her face, as if I had seen it in a dream. My mother's name was Matthidia, my father's Faustinianus, my brothers' Faustinus and Faustus.

"I learned from people who knew my father that my mother had seen a vision by which she was warned: unless she left the city of Rome with her twin sons and stayed away for ten years, she and her children would perish by a miserable fate.

"Then my father, who tenderly loved his wife and sons, put them on board a ship and sent them to Athens to be educated along with slaves and servants and a sufficient supply of money. My father kept me with him since the vision had not commanded me to go with my mother. At the end of a year my father sent men to Athens with money for my mother and to find out how they were doing, but the men never returned. Again, in the third year my father sent other men with money. They finally did return in the fourth year and related they were not able to find my mother or my brothers and there was no record of them ever reaching Athens, or any one of those who had been with them.

"My father hearing this, was devastated, not knowing where to go or what to look for. He went down to the harbor and began to ask of the sailors whether any of them had seen or heard of the bodies of a mother and two little children being cast ashore anywhere, about four years ago. No one he questioned had any knowledge and they say my father became suicidal. He was so in love with my mother and the twins that he could not live any longer without resolution. When I became old enough he left me in Rome in control of the family estate under protection of guardians and set off in search of my mother and the twinns. It was his only choice as his mind and soul would never give him peace. That was the last day I ever saw or heard from my father and I know not whether he is alive or dead, but I fear he has perished, either through a broken heart or by shipwreck. That was fifteen years ago and no word has ever been heard of my mother, father or the twins."

Peter hearing this felt sympathy and said to all who were present: "If any man who is a worshipper of God had endured what this man's father had endured, people would say his Christianity was the cause of his calamities. When these things happen to unbelievers, they charge their misfortunes to fate. Fate creates miserable unloved people who are full of errors and deprived of future hope, but when the worshippers of God suffer these things, it is to cleanse them from their post born again sins and they thus suffer patient endurance knowing correction is purification for our own good. They have complete faith in a loving Father. Rejoice when, as a believer, you have afflictions! It comes from a loving heavenly Father and results in some unknown good, whether directing our present life or giving us credit for our debt before entering the new kingdom." *(Hebrews 12, 1 Peter 1:6-7,14,22)*

It was the fourth day of our stay in Tyre. Peter headed out about daybreak, and was received by many of the inhabitants, who cried out: "God have mercy upon us. God heal us!"

Peter stood on a high stone that all might see him and thus began to speak: "God, who created the heavens and the whole universe allows punishment to those He loves and wants turned to salvation. For, men do not understand why things happen to them, particularly bad things, but God knows it is for their own good, to turn them away from impiety. The devil is a power of the left hand of God and has authority to do harm to those who sin, but only if they sin. So, with great pleasure, the devil punishes us with afflictions and diseases, but by these very diseases which have been permitted to come upon you by the good providence of God, if you humble yourself and submit to God's rules, your bodies will return to a healthy state. We forget about God until we are in trouble, as most of us never hear from our children unless they are in need.

"Now, I have been told you ate at the table of demons. After Simon killed an ox he fed you in the middle of the Forum, and everyone full of wine made friends not only with the punishing unclean spirits, but also with their prince and by way of the demons in the meat, most of you were infected with sickness. The unclean spirits would never have had power over you had not you first eaten with their prince. [see demons in the food, page 236] For God, from the beginning, laid down a law that the evil one on His left hand could not have power over any man he might wish to hurt, unless such men sat down and ate at the table with him. The table on the left has animal meat killed and prepared to eat - a demon ritual, when man started killing animals to satisfy the hunger pleasures of unclean spirits. The table on the right has the body of His Son, killed and prepared to eat: the Eucharist. God only, destroying with His left hand, can quicken with His right. He only can both smite and raise the fallen.

"You were deceived by the forerunner Simon and became dead in your souls to God and were afflicted in your bodies, but now, if you repent, as I said and submit to those things which are pleasing to God, then health will return to your bodies and souls.

"The things pleasing to God are these: To pray to Him knowing that He is the giver of all things and to abstain from the table of devils. Do not taste dead flesh or touch blood and become baptized, so you are washed from all pollution and the last, do to your neighbor those good things you wish for yourself, following the last six commandments. By these you will become dear to God and will obtain healing. Otherwise in this life, your bodies will be tormented and your souls will be punished."

After Peter had spent a few days teaching and healing them all were baptized. After that all sat down together in the market places repenting their former sins and when they of Sidon heard what was happening, they did likewise. Many because of their diseases invited Peter to come to them. So, Peter did not spend many days in Tyre, but after he had instructed all its inhabitants and freed them from all manners of diseases, he founded a church and set over it as bishop one of the elders who was with him. Then we departed for Sidon, but when Simon heard that Peter was coming he straightway fled to Beirut with Appion and his friends.

As Peter entered Sidon, they brought many in couches and laid them before him and he said to them: "I, myself cannot do anything to heal you. For, I am just a mortal like your selves and subject to many evils, but I can show you the way to salvation.

"I was instructed by the Prophet of truth, the will of the one and only God, Creator of all. If men do evil, God has ordained that they shall be injured by the prince of evil. On the other hand, any men who do good deeds as God has commanded and who have believed in Him as their Physician, will have their bodies made whole and their souls held in safety.

"Some men suffer and others cure those who suffer. It is necessary to know the cause at once of the suffering and the cure. This is proved to be none other than unbelief on the part of the sufferers and faith on the part of those who cure them. For unbelief does not believe there is a God, or His judgment. Unbelief allows them to do whatever feels good and feelings are the works of spirits, influencing good or bad in your mind. Without God's rules, a person has no way to differentiate between the suggestions of good and bad spirits, so he will naturally follow the path of least resistance: the feel-good feelings and this becomes a license to sin. Then sin opens the door to demon attacks causing sufferings and afflictions of the body, but faith, believing there is a God who will sit in judgment of all men, restrains us from errors and those who do not sin are not only free from unclean spirits and sufferings, but can also put to flight unclean spirits that are causing sufferings to others.

"If anyone continues impiety till the end of life, then as soon as the soul, which is immortal, departs, it shall pay the penalty in Hell. For even the souls of the impious are immortal, though perhaps they themselves would wish them to end with their bodies. They were forewarned and the devil never made them do their deeds; they chose by their own free will their own quality of morality and therefore they will endure without end the torments of eternal fire. This knowledge is not to terrify nor upset people, but is to warn them out of love. God is just, good and unchangeable, therefore justice demands everyone be fairly treated - rewards and punishments according to their deeds in this present life. Christ has given us the ability to see and understand this heavenly knowledge, but the impious cannot see or understand this truth. They are riding in a wagon that is headed over a cliff unless they abandon their bad influences, reversing direction and heading down the trail the Lord has mapped for us to go. Such impious men are at odds with God and are unreasonable and stubborn and have a wicked disposition towards God, especially when a man is so full of himself, arrogant and thinks himself a class above other men. Such men think they are smart and know all things, when in fact they are blind ignorant fools. When ignorance is abandoned and you humble yourself you are allowed access to the Truth. Then you begin to be pleased and displeased with the same things which please and displease God. Only then will you truly be called His friend.

"For man to be ignorant of his enemy, he is destined to be destroyed. How could one defend against an attack he refuses to acknowledge, until it is too late? The evil king has circled man's soul with siege works, for every error opens a hole and allows an attacking thrust into his heart, body and soul. How naive he is standing idly by and refusing to believe there is such an attack against him, just because he cannot see the invisible enemy! He receives and feels the pain of these punishing thrusts constantly, thinking his sufferings and afflictions are just happenstance, leaving him defenseless. We must strive for the truth so we can recognize the enemy - the old serpent and his cunning suggestions, who deceives us by feelings and thoughts of the mind, we being ignorant that these thoughts are not our own. His deceptive reason creeps through our senses and beginning at the head, he glides through our inner marrow, deceiving us of a great gain, persuading our minds with false and damaging opinions of all kinds of errors so that he may pluck us from the faith of our God. Our sin is his comfort; however, the devil is not responsible. Yes, he is a bad influence, but man makes the ultimate decision and the devil cannot make you do anything, he can only put suggestions in your mind.

"So now knowing there are good deeds and evil deeds there are then two paths in the road of life. The path of the lost is very broad and very smooth and it injures men without any effort on the part of man. The other path, the path of the saved, is narrow and rugged and only requires just a little effort from those who have traveled it to the end. All deeds in life are easy on the broad and smooth path. Take anything you want without working, because there is no right or wrong and all ways of living are fine, just follow your feelings. The rugged path requires conquering and controlling many strong and overpowering desires of your body, but if one just asks and believes in faith, the 'Helper', the 'light of the world', the 'Holy Spirit', will carry him down this path to everlasting life, helping him to honor the commandments of God and following the map of this path to the new kingdom.

"These paths are presided over by unbelief and by faith. Those on the path of unbelief prefer impious pleasures and do not believe in a judgment. They care not what is pleasing to God nor do they care about a God or their own good health and welfare. They are stubborn and rebellious and do not turn from the path after being slightly punished so they continue to receive more severe punishments hoping to turn them but in the end, are destroyed forever.

"All that is required for life's journey down the rugged path to paradise is to worship Him only and trust only in the Prophet of truth. Become baptized and thus by this pure baptism to be born again of God by saving water and strive diligently to keep His Commandments and do His will; - become as His Son"

When we reached Beirut an earthquake had taken place and the people running to Peter said: "Help us, for we are afraid and all shall utterly perish." At the same time Simon was telling everyone that Peter was a magician and had caused the earthquake and was responsible for all the diseases and many such false charges did Simon and his friends bring against Peter. As soon as Peter calmed the people, he said laughing and with boldness: "Friends I admit that I can do, God willing, everything these men say and more. So if you do not believe what I say, I am ready to turn your city upside down."

Peter then said: "Do not converse with these sorcerers or have anything to do with them. After Peter had finished speaking, the people hunted down Simon and drove him out of town. Then they came back and Peter told them: "If I were able to cause earthquakes and do all that I wish, I assure you I would not destroy Simon and his friends because I was not sent to destroy men. I am sent to save men, because, as they are, they are already destroyed. The truth is that Simon himself is a magician, a slanderer and a minister of evil to them who know not the truth. He has been given, by the evil prince, power to bring diseases on sinners, having the sinners themselves to help him in his power over them, but I am a servant of God the Creator of all things and a disciple of His Prophet who is at His right hand. I am an apostle of the true Prophet, here to serve man if man is willing to believe and change his life to good and I have the authority to drive away the unclean spirits and their diseases. I am His second messenger of the pair. The first of the pair, Simon, is the punisher and I, the second, am the healer. By me, if you believe in Him you shall be cured." Then all kneeled and lifted their hands to heaven and prayed. By their simple prayers alone they were healed and Peter then baptized them and set over them a bishop from the elders who were with him.

We then moved on to the city of Gebal and when we arrived we were told Simon had left for Tripoli. So Peter remained a few days and healed many and educated them in the Scriptures. Then we followed in Simons tracks on to Tripoli.

When we entered Tripoli, multitudes of people greeted Peter as he was headed to his lodging and he promised the people he would speak to them the next day. Arriving at the lodge, we asked if he would partake of food and he said: "Not until everyone has settled in." After which, he went out, and having bathed in the sea, he partook of food with the ones who had entered the city days before us. Now with the day concluded, we slept.

"But we impart a secret and hidden wisdom of God, which God decreed before the ages for our glory. None of the rulers of this age understood this, for if they had, they would not have crucified the Lord of glory. But, as it is written, What no eye has seen, nor ear heard, nor can the heart of man imagine, the wonderful things God has prepared for those who love him" (1 Corinthians 2).

Scroll VIII

Awaking at the second cock-crowing, Peter found us up and moving. There were now sixteen of us. Peter himself and I Clement, Nicetas and Aquila and the twelve who had preceded us. The people were already there when we came to the place of meeting and many were tormented with unclean spirits and sufferings.

Peter began to speak: "I am here to disclose the worship of God to all who are ignorant and whose minds have been corrupted by Simon. First of all, God the Creator of all, is blameless for your sufferings because you are controlled by many unclean spirits which are causing your suffering. Therefore the justice of God has come to them who are ignorant and blame Him so you can now learn the truth and you may be pardoned.

"The only good God having made all things well, handed them over to man, who was made after His image. Man was given life by His divinity, because of the affection a Father holds for His children born of Him, wishing them to love Him and them to be loved by Him, but the children rebelled and abandoned their heavenly Father. So, out of love, He has sent a Prophet, His own Son for the salvation of the children. His Son came to show them the way which leads back to His friendship, teaching them by what deeds of men the one God and Lord of all is pleased, giving us the rules of our Father, a perpetual law to all which neither can be repealed nor done away with, destroyed or impaired - not by enemies or by any impious one or concealed in any place, but is available now to be known by all. For those who choose to obey

His commands will receive all things in abundance, the fairest of fruits, fullness of years, freedom from grief and from disease.

"The key to life now and forever is obeying God's commandments. We cannot have a fellowship with Christ nor can we love Christ, unless we are committed to obeying His rules. [see commandments page 256]

"Man at first never knew of fear, grief and disease. Everything was given to man, requiring no effort on man's part and no one had ever worked. All these blessings came from God just because man was righteous, but man turned to ingratitude by an abundance of food and luxuries and like a spoiled child, expected everything. He felt he was owed everything since he had not by his labor received good things, but received good things for his righteousness. Neither had any of them fallen into any suffering or disease, causing him to look about for the God who is able to heal him. By pride, arrogance and secure luxury, there was no love or appreciation of his Father. Therefore a just punishment fell upon man and God stopped giving man anything he wanted and from then on, man would have to work for everything.

"For of the spirits who inhabit the heaven, the angels who dwell in the lowest region, being disturbed at the ingratitude of men to God, asked that they might come into the life of men and become 'watchers' for God. Then they could convict those who had acted ungratefully towards God and might subject everyone to adequate punishment. When their request was granted, they metamorphosed themselves into every nature. Being of a more godlike substance they are able easily to assume any form. So they became precious stones and goodly pearl and the most beauteous purple and choice gold and all matter that is held in most esteem.

"And they fell into the hands of some and into the bosoms of others and allowed themselves to be stolen and they also changed themselves into beasts and reptiles and fishes and birds and into whatsoever they pleased. So now, whenever man's body acquired things by hand or mouth, the angels could enter inside of man. Once inside man they could subject the bodies of the ungrateful to punishment, but the plan backfired and the angels inside man being partakers in impious pleasures themselves were sucked into human lust. They enjoyed the pleasures a physical body can give to a non-physical spirit. So getting caught up in the pleasures of bodily lusts, they became a partner with man in cohabitation with women. O, the beauty of women can conquer even the angels of heaven! Now by becoming a part of man themselves they were defiled as angels and their first powers were stripped from them and they were thus unable to return to the first purity of their proper nature. For that first nature was of a type of fire itself and was now extinguished by the weight of lust and turned into flesh. So, they followed the impious path downward. For they themselves being now fettered and bound with man's flesh were constrained and strongly bound and were unable to ascend into the heavens ever again (The fall from heaven).

"Now, being forever trapped with man they made the best of it and let man know much secret heavenly knowledge, such as how to process the earth and retrieve gold, brass, silver, iron and the like and the arts to make use of them. They enlightened man to magic, astronomy, mathematical equations, engineering and more - things that would have never been known by the human mind alone. These angels trapped in the same body with man's soul, have given man all his inventions and technology. So man received the arts of processing metals and stones, wisdom to till the earth, to sail the sea, to build cities and define kingdoms, but from their mating with women came monstrous offspring, wild in manners, brutal to others and the world was not sufficient to satisfy their appetites. They sought and killed animals and ate them contrary to nature and against God's will, but they considered themselves blameless; since they had consumed everything else, they needed meat to feed their bodies. Almighty God rained manna upon them suited to their various tastes so they would have no excuse for their killing and eating animals, but they, on account of their bastard nature, not being pleased with purity of food, longed only after the taste of blood.

"We are all born into this world neither good or bad. We become one or the other after forming habits that become very, very, difficult to break away from. So when the angel cross-breeds started eating animals men were eager to do the same and the super humans became heroes and gods to simple man (Greek Mythology). Therefore, man wished to imitate his hero and also started eating animals, a disgusting habit that man will never give up. Well, it was a short step and not long before the crossbreeds started eating humans and man quickly followed, with the consumption of flesh like his own after having first tasted animals.

"The earth was becoming greatly defiled and all things were going from bad to worse on account of these brutal angel-man crossbreeds. God wished to cast them away like an evil leaven, lest each generation form a wicked seed, being like the one before it, learning the same impious habits. If this kept up, God's Son would have very few friends for His new kingdom to come and there would not be another man or woman raised from a baby in this corrupt world, able to qualify for the new kingdom. As time moved along it finally came to be that there was only one pious man left on earth; his name was Noah. God moved in before it was too late and mankind would become extinct forever. So He told Noah to gather his three sons, their wives and children and animals enough to repopulate the earth and to save themselves in an ark. Then God sent a great deluge of water, a flood over the whole earth - a washing, cleansing, a baptism and rebirth of a purified new world.

"All was well and good again upon God's wonderful creation, earth. Only there was one serious problem. One can destroy the body but the soul lives on. Since the soul could not be destroyed, the souls of the deceased giants were also immortal, but different and more powerful than human souls. So, a new identity was introduced unto the universe and we call them 'demons' or 'unclean spirits', a new race, along with the souls of man and the souls of angels.

"Unlike man's soul that goes to Heaven, Purgatory or hell, these new souls were stuck in their own type of limbo because they were not allowed back into heaven or purgatory. So an angel was sent by God to give this new race the law and rules that would apply to them, different from the law for man and the law for angels. The angel declared: 'The all-seeing great Creator of the universe declares to you: **You shall no longer have any control over man and you will trouble no one!! Unless any such man or women, breaks any of My commandments** . But those who keep themselves to my law not only will you not harm, but you will also do honor to them and will flee from their presence and you are not allowed to make any of the pious suffer nor will you control them. The ones who do not believe in God you may do anything you want to them, good or bad and enjoy them at your own pleasure (Angel's appointed to punish). They are all yours just as man was before the flood because they are already destroyed; it is just a matter of time. But, during their given time alive, if any of them happens to repent and become one of God's worshipers, born into God's family, a child of God's, you may no longer afflict or bother with them as long as they keep His Commandments. If any of those who worship Him go astray, either committing adultery, or practicing magic, or living impurely, or breaking any one or more of His rules, then as their punishment, God will allow them to suffer something at your will or at the hands of other men in order that they might realize their error and turn back to God. And again, if they repent and live right, you are to leave them alone according to Gods order, because His lost child has come back home.' Having charged them to this effect, the angel departed.

"Therefore the unclean spirits enter into our bodies through food we consume and things we touch, such as precious stones, gold and silver, the worst being unclean food as in eating certain animals high in unclean spirits. This is why I refuse to eat meat. I need no more influences on my mind than what I already have to deal with. This is also why we fast, because the unclean spirits being pleasure seekers using our bodies, will usually leave if we deny our bodies the pleasures of food. With these unclean spirits out of your feelings, it becomes easier to follow God's commandments. By fasting one also shows the demons who is in control of this body and this body is not commanded by impious pleasure desires, but is under my total control and will respond to what I demand of it.

"Man, today, is still ignorant of this law of the unclean spirit world. Therefore everyone who partakes with them of their table of meat is sacrificing and having fellowship with demons and such men shall become subject to demons and receive all punishment from them, as being under wicked lords, but again, only if one breaks God's rules. Mankind's ignorance of God's laws, is the reason we have been sent: to educate people so they can avoid the suffering caused by these unclean spirits and bring man back to their Creator and entrance into the new kingdom to come.

"Through man's ignorance the devil and his demons have gained control over this present earth through the mind control of man and it is now his kingdom and he is it's prince and king. When Christ our King of the future Kingdom came into this present kingdom, the devil approached Him with an offer. The king of this world proposed to our King anything He wanted in this present world and He could have rule over all the lands and people, all the gold and silver and luxuries and pleasures of any kind, because all were under the power of the present king. In exchange all our King would have to do is just become subservient to the present king: 'Worship me as your lord instead of Your Father and all your heart's desires are Yours.' But our King honors His Father too much and plus, it would have robbed Him of His future glory and fantastic eternal Kingdom to come. So the present king, in fact, had nothing to offer to compare to the inheritance our King was destined to receive - not just a wonderful kingdom but also, only subjects who loved their King; the unloving would not be allowed in. His reply to the offer: 'You shall fear the Lord your God, and Him only shall you serve.'

"The king of the impious became furious with the Good King and took on a new strategy: the pious were no longer welcome in his kingdom and he would persecute the good King and the subjects of His new kingdom for the remainder of their lives while they resided in this present evil kingdom. Defectors pledging allegiance to the good King will no longer be welcome in this present kingdom, they are unwanted guest. Such non loyal subjects will be persecuted and shunned for the rest of their short time in this evil kingdom.

"But all people, good and bad, who are ignorant of God's rules and do not know of this unseen truth, are open to attack by the king of this world and in this present life are tyrannized by sufferings and sicknesses caused by unclean spirits when errors are committed.

"So now I have come with a proposal from the good King explaining the life you must live presently and if you heed His proclamation, you shall enjoy fellowship with Him in the future eternal kingdom. Therefore do not commit murder, or adultery, or hate those whom it is not right to hate, hold grudges, or steal, or set upon any evil deeds. Not only will one be deprived of the hope of future blessings in the world to come, but in the present life, he will be subjected to evil demons and terrible sufferings, after which, be punished with eternal fire. Now then, what has been said is enough for today. Those who are afflicted with ailments remain for healing and of the others, please go in peace."

When he had thus spoken, all of them remained, some in order to be healed and others to see those who obtained cures. Peter laid his hands upon all who wanted and praying, healed them proclaiming "go and sin no more". Everyone blessed and thanked God and believed in the message Peter brought. Then everyone departed to their homes with an invitation to come back the next day and when all had left we together partook of food, the body and blood of our Lord and then headed off to bed.

"And I am convinced that nothing can ever separate us from God's love. Neither death nor life, neither angels nor demons, neither our fears for today nor our worries about tomorrow—not even the powers of hell can separate us from God's love. No power in the sky above or in the earth below—indeed, nothing in all creation will ever be able to separate us from the love of God that is revealed in Christ Jesus our Lord" (Romans 8).

Scroll IX

On the next day, Peter went out with his companions and coming to the former place, took his stand and proceeded to say: "As I spoke to you yesterday, God cut off by water all the impious men, having found only one alone amongst all men who was pious and caused him to be saved in an ark with his three sons and their wives and children.

"Therefore the greatest impiety of all is forsaking the sole Lord of all and worshipping any of His creations, as though they can do anything for you -angels, men, governments, planets, money or objects of good luck. There is only One invisible unseen God; Love Him with all your heart, soul and mind.

"That serpent also influences our desire for images of God. We adore hand-made visible images in honor of the invisible God. Now this is most certainly an error, because things created by man and given honor are gods and idols whether worshipped as themself or worshipped as representatives of the unseen world. God specifically said that nothing fashioned of human hands should be at His place of worship. (Exodus 20:25, Isaiah 17:8) If one really wished to worship the image of God, he would do good to man and thus worship the true image of God, for the image of God is every man. If we truly want to honor the image of God, then we should pay honor and reverence to man who is made in the image of God and show mercy to man as God has shown mercy to us. Show mercy to the image of God and resolve disputes immediately, never holding grudges, because that puts one at odds with God. Resolve any hard feelings before the sun sets and give food to the hungry, drink to the thirsty and clothing to the naked, hospitality to the stranger and necessary things to the prisoner. That is what will be regarded as true worship bestowed upon God. All these things we do for our fellow man go to the honor of God's image. The person who neglects these things disgraces the divine image and anyone who commits murder, adultery, or anything that causes suffering or injury to men, has violated the image of God. It is the serpent lurking inside that convinces that there is nothing wrong with injuring certain people.

"After the flood, Noah continued to live three hundred and fifty years with all of his descendants in peace and harmony, being the only patriarch, since there was no one of his stature left alive to give him competition. After Noah's death, his three sons were each ambitious, lusting for the kingdom and being eager to reign, each one competing against the other for control. One attempted it by war, another by deceit, another by persuasion. One of these was of the family of Ham, whose descendants became the Egyptians and Babylonians and Persians.

"Of this family there was born in due time a certain one, Nemrod, who re- introduced the demons magical practices which are in opposition to God. Him the Greeks have called Zoroaster - a master of sorcery, magic and astrology. He, being ambitious to rule over all and being a great magician, attempted to compel the wicked one to make him supreme ruler over mankind. A magician commanding the evil king's demons was permitted, but who did he think he was, commanding the king himself? Therefore, the wicked one, being a prince and having authority over Zoroaster who attempted to compelled him, wrathfully poured out the fire of the kingdom that he might both bring to allegiance and punish Zoraster who at first tried to constrain him.

Our God is long-suffering but the evil prince is not long-suffering and took great offence at this arrogant little human and set him, Zoraster, on fire with a lightning strike.

"The people buried the remains of his body and honored his burial place with a temple among the Persians, where the descent of the fire occurred and worshipped him as a god. Others were also buried there who died by lightning and as time passed, this became a habit, to honor the dead with temples, statues and lighted altars, making them out to be gods.

"These man made images became representatives of their gods, a god being anything that would care for them and lead them through life, give them birth, jobs, food, healthcare, protection from enemies and supply the rest of their needs and desires. Therefore, people abandoned again the unseen all powerful one and only God of all creation. This foolish knowledge was given to them by the evil intelligence of the magicians, leading them to errors of worship and by magical ceremonies, they assigned them feasts with sacrifices, libations, flutes, and shouting's, by means of which senseless men, being deceived and their kingdom being taken from them, loved the new worship they had adopted. They preferred the pleasures of error, before truth.

"So here 'we' are as good merchantmen, bringing the Truth of the One and only God, the Creator, back to you. If therefore, you acknowledge and accept us, you shall be able to escape the demons, disciples of the present kingdom's prince and the sufferings which are inflicted by those unclean spirits therefore putting them to flight. You then gain back control over them and your body, instead of their controlling you.

"On the other hand, you are oppressed by strange sufferings inflicted by unclean spirits and when the body dies, you shall have your souls also punished forever; not by God's inflicting vengeance, but because it is the law for man and just judgment for evil deeds.

"For the unclean spirits, after entering the body gain power over the unrighteous and eventually become blended with the impious souls and after the body dissolves back into the earth whence it originally came, the soul being united to the demon travels with it into whatever places it pleases. And what is most terrible of all, when at the end of all things the unclean spirit is first consigned to the purifying fire, the soul which is mixed with it is under the necessity of being horribly punished, but the demon has won and accomplished his goal. For the soul, being made of light and not capable of bearing the flame of fire, is tortured, but the demons soul, being in the substance of his own kind, is greatly pleased, becoming the strong chain of the soul that he has swallowed up. The reason why the unclean spirits delight in entering into men's bodies is this. Being spirits and having desires after meats and drinks and sexual pleasures, but not being able to partake of these by reason of their being spirits, they need man's physical organs for their enjoyment, so they enter into the bodies of men. Now by just persuading the mind of man to physically act on their desires, they may obtain the pleasures that they wish, whether it be meat with blood by means of men's teeth, or sexual pleasure by means of men's members. Yet they can only persuade not force man to indulge in their pleasures and if such ignorant men give in to their desires, the physical bodies of the men will later be afflicted by demon punishments and this is why so many of you are suffering sickness. These unclean spirits can enter our bodies from the food we eat and most assuredly, through meat. That is why we were given the rules for unclean meat. The unclean is noted as such because it has more unclean spirits and pork being the most contaminated of all since pigs are the demons pleasure animal of choice, second only to man. (Matthew 8:31)

"Therefore, in order to resist and suppress these demons and encourage them to leave the body, one needs to deprive them of their pleasures and the use of one's body for their desires. The most useful tools for this purpose are **abstinence and fasting -** denying the body the demons pleasures. For, if they enter into men's bodies for the sake of sharing pleasures, it also works in reverse and most of them will abandon you if you make the body reject their desires, since they are pleasure seekers for their spirit and gain satisfaction by using the human body. If you do not participate in promiscuous sex they will leave you and find someone who will satisfy them and the same thing happens if you 'fast' and deny yourself meat and food. They love eating the flesh of animals since it was a pleasure they started man doing in the first place. Our Teacher, The Christ, fasted for forty days before His temptation by the devil in order to rid His human body of any unclean spirit influence and show the devil Who was in control of this human body. Moses also fasted forty days when he transcribed the Ten Commandments so he could give God's word uninterrupted attention. 'Is this not the fast which I choose, to loosen the bonds of wickedness, to undo the bands of the yoke, and to let the oppressed go free and break every yoke? (control the purity of our bodies) Is it not to divide your bread with the hungry and bring the homeless poor into the house....remove the yoke from your midst... the pointing of the finger and speaking wickedness...' (Isaiah 58:6)

"Unclean spirits, just like all of us, have different personalities. After all, before the flood, they were part human. Their personalities reflect our impious traits: blasphemy, pride and arrogance, back stabbing, jealousy, murder, theft, anger, fear, and so on and as with people, some personalities are stronger than others and of a more malignant kind which can remain in the body undergoing punishment, though they are punished with it; therefore it is needful to have recourse to God by prayers and petitions along with fasting, cutting off all impurity in order for God to heal. (Mark 9:29)

"But it is necessary in our prayers to give thanks to God for His help in a difficult situation. For all afflictions and blessings are done to the believer, more than to the unbeliever. Therefore the unclean spirits themselves, knowing the amount of faith of those of whom they take possession, measure their stay proportionately. Wherefore they stay permanently with the unbelieving, tarry for a while with the weak in faith, but with those who thoroughly believe and who do good keeping God's commandments they cannot remain even for a moment and they will leave and go find a body where they can enjoy their impious pleasures. A soul turned by faith into the nature of water, quenches the demon as a spark of fire.

"Therefore the goal of every one should be putting to flight or gaining control over his own demons. For, being mixed up with men's souls they suggest to every one's mind desires and pleasures they like, causing him to be distracted and neglect his salvation.

"Many not knowing how their minds are influenced, consent to the evil thoughts suggested by the unclean spirits, as if they came up with the idea on their own. One would never know, because we have been trained by society that demons do not exist and if anyone says they do, he becomes an outcast person, to be shunned and avoided. Thus people never realize they are held captive and the demons that lurk in their bodies deceive man into thinking it is not a demon that is distressing them, but just fate or an illness that is remedied by psychotherapy, medicine or surgery.

"So that the unclean spirit can deny his existence, he trains people's minds to ignore and hate us, the bringers of truth and so people stay deceived, not knowing why their health is failing, for we cannot force a people against their will to accept our word. They conceal from many that they are unclean spirits, but they cannot fool us who have been educated by our Lord to their invisible mystery.

"God does not take vengeance directly upon impious souls, but His whole creation rises up and inflicts punishments upon the impious. Although in this present world the goodness of God bestows good on the pious and the impious alike, the rest of His creation - His earth, moon, planets, stars, winds and waters is not so long-suffering and it quickly becomes wearied by the crimes of the wicked and will blight the crops of the earth, or change the composition of the air; the heat of the sun is increased beyond measure, or there is an excessive amount of rain or of cold and pestilence and famine and death in various forms. For the creature hastens to take vengeance on the wicked. Yet the goodness of God restrains it and bridles its indignation against the wicked and compels it to be obedient to His mercy, rather than to be inflamed by the sins and the crimes of men. The patience of God waits for the conversion of men as long as they are in this present kingdom.

"For God is almighty good, righteous and long-suffering and He waits on those who might repent of the evils they are doing and start living 'good' and then receive a reward on the 'day of judgment'.

"By this good knowledge, begin to obey God and to oppose the evil demon lusts and thoughts persuading your mind and feelings that you may be able to recover the original salvation that was given to humanity. Then blessings will straightway come upon you and when you receive them, you will refrain from the trial of evils. Give blessings and thanks to the true Giver, being King of peace forever and giver of unspeakable good things. Wash in a flowing river or fountain or even in the sea, with the invoking of the Father, Son and Holy Spirit. Drive away evil spirits lurking inside you, resisting their evil pleasure desires by keeping God's rules. You have become a 'child of God', so keep the commandments and unclean spirits will flee from you and then you rejoice the more because, through grace, your name has been written in heaven and the Holy Spirit and angels rejoice with you because you have overcome evil.

"Moses gave man the Old Covenant. It used Moses' laws to force man to keep the commandments of God, but with unclean spirits inside man from the food man ate, it never worked. The demon influence on the inside was stronger than the fear of punishment from the outside.

"So our Christ instituted a New Covenant. First, fast so the unclean spirits will leave or know who is in control. Then, 'Eat

My flesh and drink My blood,' often. I, the Holy Spirit, am now inside of you and will help you overcome the demons. With the Holy Spirit inside, you will love and desire to do your Father's will and keep His rules, from love within, instead of from force without.

"Be sure to fill your body with the Holy Spirit or the unclean spirit will return and might bring more with him making you worse off than before.

"The unclean spirits now have no power over you, unless, of your own free will, you choose to become their slave again. Worship God and keep Him inside of you. The 'Helper' will make it more desirable to remain chaste and righteous, devoting yourselves as much as you can to the perfection of purity."

Peter had finished talking for the day and asked those to approach who were distressed with diseases and he laid his hands upon them and prayed, and immediately they were healed. Then the crowds dispersed.

When we arrived at our lodging, the headmaster of the lodge insisted we stay in his house where beds were spread and everything was waiting for us. When Peter refused, the wife of the man pleaded with Peter, but Peter still declined until their daughter came out, bound with chains. The man and his wife were startled. Their daughter had been locked in a closet, having been for a long time possessed with an unclean spirit. She fell at Peter's feet and begged him to stay and Peter asked: "What is the meaning of her chains?" Her parents were thunderstruck with astonishment and could not speak, but a servant said: "This girl has been possessed of a demon since she was seven and she would scream out of control and bite people and was abusive to anyone who came close to her. She has been possessed for twenty years until now, when you appeared. No one has ever cured her or approached her, for she had brutally assaulted people since she was stronger than any man. For the first time, she has control of her senses. Just by your presence, the unclean spirit has left." Peter helped her remove the chains from her hands and feet and agreed to remain with them. Then Peter's wife and the rest of us came on in. Everyone received a separate bedroom and after having taken food in the usual manner and given praises to God, we all went to sleep.

"Do not let this Book of the Law depart from your mouth; meditate on it day and night, so that you may be careful to do everything written in it. Then you will be prosperous and successful. (Joshua 1).

Scroll X

Peter rose early and went out into the garden, where there was
a large pond into which a stream of water constantly flowed and
after bathing and praying, he sat down. Then one of our people
came in and said a large crowd was assembling outside. Peter
said to let them in and got up. After moving to a convenient spot,
he started to speak: "God, having formed the heaven and the
earth and having made all things in them, He made man. Man
was righteous and had no pain and suffering, but when man
sinned, as I explained the last two days, he became subject to all
suffering and was deprived of blessings. It was not reasonable for
the Giver and Creator of all to be treated with such disrespect.
Man could no longer be allowed all the wonderful gifts while
being so ungrateful, but because of Gods abundant mercy, He
sent His Son, the Prophet and the Prophet has come to all of us
who are ignorant, to instruct us what to do and how to live and to
bring back worship and glory to the One who deserves it and who
loves us all - the Creator of all things, the Giver of all blessings.
But you must choose of your own 'free will' and if you choose to
receive God in your minds and hearts, you will have great things
in this present life and you will also receive eternal blessings in
the future life - a future kingdom on earth as it presently is in
heaven.

"Once you receive God in your hearts and minds you will be
given the power of the Holy Spirit, 'The Helper', to help you
keep His commandments, which is necessary. As a result of
being one of God's children, you will continue to be attacked by
the unclean spirits, but you now have the knowledge of them and

their evil goals. With the help of the Holy Spirit you now have the power to resist and keep these evil beasts away. Also the fear of just punishment will help motivate you to stay on the right path. You can say to the horrible serpent which lurks in your heart, 'The Lord God you shall fear, and Him alone you shall serve by obeying His commandments.' On every account it is advantageous to fear God alone, a just and righteous God - the only One man can trust to be fair to all. With man's governments there is no fairness and some men are wrongfully punished and other men do evil deeds and are not punished at all. As long as men have jealousy, envy and lust, there will be injustice and man's governments become unreliable. But with a righteous One, you will only be deservingly punished and only if breaking His rules. The just government of God holds no favoritism, nor inequity.

"Therefore, you who at first were made to be rulers and lords of all things, approach with confidence to God. Those who have His image as their bodies, have in like manner the likeness of His judgment in their minds. Before, by acting like irrational animals, you have lost your souls, becoming like swine - the prey of unclean spirits. If, therefore, you receive the law of God, you become men again. For it cannot be said to irrational animals: 'You shall not kill, you shall not commit adultery, you shall not steal, you shall not wrongfully desire the property of another'. Therefore do not refuse when invited, to return to your first nobility. For it is possible, if you be conformed to God by the good works He requires, you shall be reinstated as lords of all.

"Most important for everyone is the constant daily learning - reading or hearing the Word of truth. Man's soul needs daily repetition and recharging otherwise he quickly forgets and wanders astray. This is also why you will need daily fellowship with each other - to speak the Word and reinforce each other. One must continually grow and strengthen his faith, just as one has to feed the unclean spirits with evil pleasures or they will leave, the Holy Spirit thrives on the Word of God and loves to reside inside a body that is constantly being fed the Word. Man must hear or read the Word over and over daily for the rest of his life because memory is short, wishy-washy and fickle and the 'Word' is life-sustaining spiritual food. You have to have it daily, or your spirit could wither and die. Just as earthly food is necessary, daily, for the survival of your physical body, the 'Word' must be fed to your soul and spirit. Therefore keep constant fellowship with other believers reinforcing each other because the evil king is always on the prowl and will devour those who are weak in the Word. So keep your defenses strong by daily absorbing the Word and its inspiration, Divine guidance and influence.

"God exercises patience because He is merciful and gracious and He foresees that many of the ungodly become godly and will be converted to God, given time, forsaking their sins and doing good works. Therefore everyone is allowed time for his consideration of good and evil - time to choose good or evil, acquiring rewards or bringing destruction on themselves.

"God insists that one hold to patience and gentleness to prevent the inroads of anger and do not envy or hold hard feelings of any kind, but be content with your own possessions, not lusting for what belongs to another or coveting your neighbor's belongings. Not even when driven by poverty should you plunder the goods of others, but in all things observe justice because without these Godly morals, you invite unclean spirits to you and of your own accord give them the power to inflict pain, suffering, sickness, madness, lust and unlawful love.

"Lust, envy and jealousy are the root of all impieties and birth murders, adulteries, thefts and all forms of evils and wickedness. While you indulge in unrighteousness you give to wicked spirits an opportunity of ruling and obtaining authority over you. For when they invade your senses, they influence their joy which is lust, injustice and cruelty and compel you to be obedient to things that excite their pleasures and at the same time rejoicing, while wreaking your bodies and your soul. God indeed, permits you to suffer this at their hands by a certain righteous judgment He originally decreed, hoping, that from these very afflictions, one would by his own will, change the direction of his life, realizing how horrific it is to be subject to unclean spirits and not to the loving God whom they have forsaken.

"By guarding against sinning, we guard against suffering"
(Clement of Alexandria).

"Punishment in the present life of those who worship God is inflicted upon them, out of love for sins into which they have fallen, just as we punish our children if they disobey our rules. Some children require more punishment than others, but we could never ever fail to love them, no matter how badly they behave.

"My son, do not regard lightly the discipline of the Lord nor faint when you are reproved by Him; for those whom the Lord loves He disciplines and He scourges every son whom He receives. It is for discipline that you endure; God deals with you as with sons; for what son is there whom his father does not discipline? But if you are without discipline.... then you are illegitimate children

and not sons. ....He disciplines us for our good, so that we may share His holiness. All discipline for the moment seems not to be joyful, but sorrowful; yet to those who have been trained by it, afterwards it yields the peaceful fruit of righteousness" (Hebrews 12).

"As people finish this present life, such sufferings will have extracted from them the debt due for errors committed since they were born again and then at death they will be freed, at least in half, from the eternal punishments which are there prepared. All the trials and tribulations in your life now, but only if you are a believer, a child of God's, will it be considered at judgment as full or partial payment.

"But those that do not acknowledge God or believe in a judgment, being bound by the pleasures of the present life, will be shut out from eternal good things at the time of their death.

"If not convinced that what we say is true, do not become upset at us because we announce the things which we consider to be good because we are commanded to tell everyone, knowing only a few will make it to the new kingdom."

Having said this he asked the demoniacs and those taken with diseases, to approach him. As they came, he laid his hands on them, and prayed, and dismissed them healed. Peter then reminded them to come and attend every day while he was there.

After the people left we all rested under the shade of a large tree and partook of food. Then Peter permitted us to ask questions and there were twenty of us putting all kinds of questions to him and he answered them all. After a short day evening had finally come, so we all went back to the house and slept.

"Brothers and sisters, join with others in following my example. Pay close attention to those who live in keeping with the pattern we gave you.

I have told you those things many times before. Now I say it again with tears in my eyes. Many people live like enemies of the cross of Christ. The only thing they have coming to them is death. Their stomach is their god. They brag about what they should be ashamed of. They think only about earthly things.

But we are citizens of heaven. And we can hardly wait for a Savior from there. He is the Lord Jesus Christ. He has the power to bring everything under his control. By his power he will change our earthly bodies. They will become like his glorious body" (Philippians 3).

Scroll XI

Peter rising and finding us awake did his usual routine; bathed and prayed as we did also. When the crowd had come, he started to speak: "Before I gave you the truth, you learned many religions which have rooted hurtful conceptions, so it may take time to purify your minds. While the good seed of the true word has been planted, beware not to choke it out with the evil cares you had before, but move on in good works accumulating rewards which will be waiting for you in the new kingdom.

"You are the image of the invisible God and he who wishes to be pious towards God does good to man, because the body of man bears the image of God. Everything good done to man by you may be accounted as good works done to God. Give honor to the image of God by giving food to the hungry, drink to the thirsty, clothing to the naked, care to the sick, shelter to the stranger and visiting him who is in prison. Put others above yourselves and do not damage the image of God committing murder, adultery, stealing and dishonoring him with any actions, which grieves man.

"In all the cities I go many say to me: 'God should have made us good in the first place.' And I explain: God did make you good it is man's free will that created evil. If God forced you good, it would not have been your choice and you would be nothing but an unhappy slave without freedom and could never love your Creator by your own free choice. Therefore this freedom of will brings forth good or evil on its own through the decisions of man.

"Before knowing the truth, you were easily seduced by temporary earthly pleasures and that keeps you from eternal things. So we explain to you the promises that belong to piety, so that by good deeds you may inherit with us the griefless world.

"You must abandon that evil serpent that lurks in you who at first promised man knowledge but instead brought death and destruction into the world.

"The unclean spirits love to dwell in the bodies of men that they may fulfill their own desires, compelling men to obey their own lusts. If you allow them to be your master you eventually become completely their vessels and your soul bonds with theirs as one (possessed). This is what happened to Simon, who is now seized with such disease that he is totally lost and cannot be healed. That unclean spirit is there because Simon desired it and has allowed it to be so imbedded in his soul that if any one tried to drive it out, it could kill his body and the authorities could charge us with murder."

I, Clement, was still composing these scrolls as we listened to Peter speak. Peter talked about purifying your heart - cleaning up the inside, the part of a person God has to look at. Therefore do not become so concerned about the outside, your appearance, the part men look at and care about. Do not concern yourself with what other people think of you, only care what your Lord thinks.

Then Peter discussed genesis, fate and happen-chance vs. the providence of God. There is no spontaneous, verbal or bodily behavior done unconsciously since most actions come by free choice, from interaction of human souls with spirits within the body, good or bad. All other actions are performed by the divine Creator - Providence guiding human destiny.

After Peter was finished he ministered to many and later baptized them in the fountains which are near the sea. Then Peter set up a bishop, twelve elders and deacons. We all bid farewell and proceeded on our quest. In one day we traveled from Tripoli to Antioch and finally settled in at Orthas for the evening.

The next day Peter had Nicetus and Aquila go on ahead of us into the Gentile cities to scout them out ahead of our arrival. After they had left, someone urged Peter, while we were so close, to check out the island of Arvad to see some spectacular works of art. Peter agreed, as he was very courteous and said he would very much enjoy that. So the following day we reached the island by ship in an hour's time and headed to see the wonderful carved wooden columns that were inside a temple.

After we had admired the columns we headed over to see the great paintings, but as we were leaving the columns Peter encountered a poor beggar woman at the entrance asking money from those going in. Peter approached her and said: "Tell me, woman, what is your problem? Why do you beg for money and not work for it with the hands God has given you?"

She responded: "Look at my hands, they are no longer hands. They have been destroyed by my chewing on them."

Then Peter asked perplexed: "Why would you chew on your hands?"

She said: "I have lost my reason for existing and do not have the courage to put an end to my miserable life of pain and suffering."

Peter responded: "In your case the suffering is self-inflicted. Do you think that those who destroy themselves are set free from torments? Those who kill themselves subject their souls to greater punishments."

She said: "I wish I knew for sure that all souls continue on after death because that would indeed give me the strength I am desperately in need of to kill myself. I would be willing to suffer any torment just to be able to see the souls of my precious children, even for but an hour."

Then Peter replied: "What has happened to you O' woman to even consider such a dreadful punishment? Souls do indeed continue on after this life, but be sure you live on in paradise and not in Hell. Tell me the cause of your suffering and I can give you a remedy, so your life will come to an end without torment."

Then the woman became silent, her mind churning way back in time, trying to recollect. She finally replied: "I was born a child of very noble parents, blood relatives of the Emperor." She became quiet again, then continued: "When I turned fourteen years of age, I became the wife of a powerful man. We first had two sons who were twins and later we had another son. My husband's brother, also a powerful man, became obsessed and violently inflamed with lust towards me. I, unlike all the other women I knew, valued chastity above all things and refused to consent to his aggressive advances. While I was resisting my brother in law, I would never dare disclose to my husband this disgusting behavior of his brother because that would have just set brother against brother and disgraced the entire royal family. Of course, who would believe me anyway - a lustful young mother? So, I decided the best solution was for me to leave the country for a period of time until his brothers passions subsided. It was my presence that was inflaming his desires and my only solution was to leave, taking the twins and leaving the younger son with his father.

"Because my family was so religious, I pretended that I had a dream in which Juno stood by me in a vision and told me that I should immediately depart from the city with the twins and should be absent until Juno should command me to return. If I did not do so, I would perish with all my children. And so it was done. For as soon as I told the dream to my husband, he was terrified. Thus sending with me my twin sons and also slaves and maid servants and giving us plenty of money, we sailed for Athens where there I might educate my sons and stay until I felt it appropriate to return. After two days in route the seas raised up, yet the weather was calm and clear. I will never forget how strange that was. Within seconds a wave larger than the ship broke over the side. Everyone quickly took to security in great confusion. The crew was struggling to turn the bow into the waves not knowing which direction they were coming from. Everything happened so fast I never even had time to think of my boys nor did fear enter my mind. The ship heaved completely out of the water as if the entire sea was vanished out from under us. Coming back down it hit the next wave so hard, the entire ship split from front to back and collapsed within itself. The last I remember was the powerful wave snatching me out of the sinking debris under my feet. Then I remember lying on a large rock as the day was dawning. It was still very calm and I was certainly just dreaming. The sky was clear and the sun began to feel wonderful on my body. As I raised and looked around panic hit me. My mind started screaming: 'this is a dream, this is just a dream!' What little clothes I had left on my body were shredded, but I had not a mark on my being. Looking all around there was nothing to be seen but miles of barren coast. I stood and started to move along the rocky shoreline, slowly my memory began coming back together. Where are my children? I was paralyzed. Looking everywhere there was no sign of anything, ship, people, bodies, nothing! The whole day was spent wandering back and forth down the shore line. Then, finally I saw some live bodies, only to discover they were local people and not from our ship.

"I told them all I could remember and they felt my sorrow and frustration and helped me search for any sign of my boys. A woman tried her best to comfort me but I was too devastated to respond to any affection. She tried to tell me of the misfortunes of others in order to comfort me, but it only made things worse because I could not regard the misfortunes of others as comfort. Many offered to take me into their homes, but all I wanted was for life to end there and then. Finally, a certain poor women convinced me to stay with her. She spoke to me of her husband who was a sailor and had vanished at sea while still a young man. Many men had since asked for her in marriage, but she never recovered from the man she lost and preferred widowhood through love of her husband. She offered, 'we shall share whatever we can gain by the labor of our hands.' So I willingly conceded on account of the faithful affection which she retained for her husband. Not long after, my hands long torn with gnawing, became powerless and she who had taken me in fell into palsy. Now she just lies at home in her bed. The affection of those women who had formerly pitied me grew cold and they now ignore me. We are both helpless. Now I beg for anything that would serve two wretches.

"I should stop boring you with such a long story about my own personal grief's and not detain you from your friends any longer. You have heard enough of my pitiful life so give me your promise, the remedy by which both of us may end our miserable lives without torment."

While she was speaking, Peter had become very engrossed in her story and stood there staring in silence. At the same time, I Clement, came up and said: "I have been seeking you everywhere. I should have known, only you would find people more interesting than the finest art work in the world – God's creation preferred over man's." Peter instructed me to head on back to the ship and there wait on him. Then Peter turned back to the woman struck with wonder and said: "Just several more questions and I will give you your remedy. Where were you from? What is your name and your husband and sons'?"

She said: "I was an Ephesian and my husband a Sicilian," instead of telling Peter they were all Romans. And she also gave false names to her family.

Then Peter, supposing that she had answered truly said: "Well! For a great time there I thought something incredible was about to happen and I was becoming very suspicious you were a certain woman."

She responded: "Tell me of such a woman that I might learn of one more wretched than myself."

Then Peter said: "There is a certain young man among those with me who has become a part of our faith and was a Roman citizen. He told me of a father, a mother, and twin brothers who disappeared and he has never heard from them for twenty years.

His mother had a vision that forced her to leave Rome or face a horrible fate. So she left Rome for Greece with just the twins. Anyway the story goes on and I will stop there because it is irrelevant." Peter was taken aback when he looked upon her. Something had changed her countenance as though life itself had been given to the dead.

She said: "Please, I beg, continue."

Peter continued: "Surely, anything to help a lost soul. Let's see; O yes, I believe I said, his mother had a vision. She told his father a deity had warned her of a terrible fate that would befall her family if she did not immediately leave Rome. So it was agreed and she left Rome for Greece with just the two twins, along with servants, leaving the youngest son in Rome with his father. His mother and brothers were never heard from again and his father was struck with so much grief and with time realized he would never recover, so he left to find them or spend the remainder of his life searching for them. He felt that was his only option. The other was to live idly in pain and anguish, so his father left and was never heard from again. At least, he felt his father satisfied a dying soul that could have never endured a tortuous slow death. That was twenty years ago. Since then he....."

Before Peter had finished telling the story the woman lost the color in her face. Peter grabbed her and held her up, giving her comfort. When she started to recover, Peter inquired, as to what happened. With difficulty, recovering her breath and brushing her face, she said: "Is he here, the young man of whom you speak?" But Peter, realizing what was happening, said: "Tell me first or else you shall not see him."

Then she said: "I am the mother of the youth."

Then Peter said: "What is his name?"

And she answered: "Clement."

Peter responded: "Well, this might be a wonderful day the Lord has made after all. It is he, the one who spoke with me a little while ago, whom I directed to go back to the ship." She attempted to stand but fell back against Peter's shoulder. She insisted Peter hasten her to the ship.

Peter said: "Patience O' woman, all things will happen in their due time. You must first promise me, you will do exactly as I say."

She said: "I will do anything, just show me my only son."

Peter replied: "When you have seen him, keep it to yourself until we leave the island."

She answered: "I will do anything you say."

Peter took her by the hand and led her to the boat. But I, seeing him leading the woman by the hand, laughed at the sight of the two - Peter bringing back a wobbly old beggar woman. It seems that everywhere we go, he always brings home someone in need. So I hurried to them and offered to lead her instead of him, but as soon as I touched her hand she straightened up quickly and embraced me violently, trying to kiss me. I shook her off as if a madwoman and was somewhat disturbed with Peter. But, through my respect for Peter, I checked myself.

Peter said: "Oh Clement, my son, do not push away your mother." Now I really was disturbed with Peter, as I did not appreciate this kind of humor, but at the same time the words stabbed my memory as I was staring at the old beggar woman. Then, she spoke and my mind and soul were paralyzed, unable to speak or move. I was frozen in time, my mind rapidly recalling what little I remembered of her countenance in my memory. The longer I gazed, the more familiar it grew to me. My mother! As others had been watching all this unfold, they moved in closer in unbelief. I, a wealthy man, was the son of the woman who begs?

Peter broke the silence: "Clement, where are your manners, honor your mother - say hello."

My mother said: "Son, take your time, I know the sight of me is disturbing."

I responded: "Not at all, I just never had a mother and do not know what to say or do."

She replied: "That's fine. It will take a little time for both of us." She then turned to Peter and said: "Before we leave I should bid farewell to the woman who took me in for she is poor and paralytic and bedridden." When Peter and all who were present heard this, they admired the goodness of the woman and immediately Peter ordered some to go and to bring the woman in her bed as she lay. And when she had been brought and placed in the presence of all, Peter said: "I am a preacher of truth, for confirming the faith of all those who stand by, that they may know and believe that there is one God, who made heaven and earth. In the name of Jesus Christ, His Son, let this woman rise." And as soon as he had said this, she arose.

By then the crowd of locals which had gathered around us were astounded by what Peter was doing. So Peter addressed them briefly explaining the faith of a God none had ever heard of, then added that if they wished to know more, they should come to Antioch, where we would be staying for three months, teaching fully the things of salvation. "For if men leave their country and their parents for commercial or military purposes, they would be benefited beyond measure to visit us for any amount of time they could afford since their reward was eternal life". After Peter had spoken, I presented a thousand drachmas to the woman who had let my mother live in her house and committed her to the care of a certain good man, the chief person in that town, who promised that he would gladly do what we asked of him. I also distributed a little money among some others and among those women who had formerly comforted my mother in her miseries. I also expressed my thanks and after this we sailed, along with my mother to Antaradus.

After we arrived and had partaken of food, the Eucharist, and given thanks, we had some extra time so I said to Peter: "It seems the woman that took my mother in has done a work of philanthropy."

And Peter answered: "You think so? The woman who received your mother after her shipwreck would not be considered philanthropic because she was motivated by pity for a woman who had been shipwrecked, grieving for her children, naked, destitute, hungry and greatly in need. Your mother would have been received by anyone. Even the impious would have felt pity for her. And after we rescued your mother, she repaid the woman out of friendship, not philanthropy. There is much difference between friendship and philanthropy, because friendship springs from something received or given in return, referred to as compensation. You do something for me I will do something for you, but philanthropy loves and benefits every man as the giver expecting nothing in return, including praise or acknowledgement before other men. Had your mother been the woman's enemy, she could have been called philanthropic."

Then I asked: "Wouldn't you think that being a stranger she would have been philanthropic who did good to someone she did not know?"

Then Peter said: "Compassionate indeed, I will call her. It would be similar to the feelings and care a mother has for her children, a natural instinct."

Then I asked: "By what deeds then, can anyone be philanthropic?"

And Peter answered: "He is the philanthropic man who does good even to his enemies. He who practices philanthropy is an imitator of God, doing good to the righteous and the unrighteous, as God Himself graciously grants His sun and His heavens to all in the present world, but if you just do 'good' to the good, but not to the evil, you undertake to do the work of a judge and you do not strive for philanthropy. We are not to judge while in this temporary kingdom, but to educate and offer salvation for the next kingdom because when this kingdom ends, the Good Judge will arrive with a sword. The Prophet of the truth said: 'Good things are ordained to come to man and blessed is he by whom they come; in like manner evil things must also come to man, but woe to the judgment coming to him through whom they come.'

"By God-ordained, free choice we can be good or evil and this, in most part, does not come from the providence of God, but is only peculiar to the free will God allowed us to have. We are all in a war, the battle for the wonderful new kingdom. If one, by his own choice, chooses to be good, he will be in heavy combat while he is in this present evil kingdom. So, by the judgment of God, he who survives the battle by staying good and is found blameless is deemed worthy of eternal life and for the good man who continues the battle for goodness, he will be challenged and tempted by those who, by their own free will, continue in evil. Through the persecution by the evil soldiers you will be hated, slandered, plotted against, struck, cheated, accused, tortured and disgraced in hopes of breaking your struggle for the ultimate treasure.

"But the Master knows that those who wrongfully do these things are ignorant and do not realize what they are doing because men who break the commandments of God are allowed to be manipulated by the spirit of wickedness. They are men who have become instruments of wickedness through sin and are unknowingly slaves of the evil one. Therefore God has given to His disciples philanthropy, so we will not take offence from their actions toward us and will actually try to rescue these lost souls from the evil one and eternal torment in Hell. We do not resist these impious men or try to get revenge, for we feel sorry for them. If they only knew what was eagerly awaiting them at the end, they would immediately sober up: a fate more gruesome than any revenge man's mind could ever conceive. It is natural to all to love those who love them, but the righteous man tries also to love his enemies and to bless those who slander him and even to pray for his enemies and to be compassionate to those who do him wrong. Having devoted himself to love his neighbor as himself, he is not afraid of poverty, but becomes poor by sharing his possessions with those who have none. This perfect love towards every man is the male part of philanthropy, but the female part of it is compassion, to feed the hungry, to give drink to the thirsty, to clothe the naked, to visit the sick and to take in the stranger, in short, to have compassion on him who is in misfortune."

But I, Clement, said: "That is impossible to do - to do good to your enemies, putting up with all their insolences and immaturity; I do not think it ever to be possible with humans."

Then Peter answered: "You have spoken O' so truly. For philanthropy takes a divine amount of discipline and self-control to obtain and help from the Holy Spirit."

Then I said: "How then is it possible to do?"

Peter answered: "O' beloved Clement, the way to get it is this. Everyone should understand that the ill treatment and abuse that comes from his enemies is of the greatest benefit he can receive for his salvation. We believers, forgiven for all our past unrighteousness and born again, will all eventually get to the new kingdom just on our faith and the mercy of our loving Father. But since we are still imperfect we slip in our quest for God's will and break commandments, usually unintentionally. Therefore with a just and fair Father, treating everyone with equality, we will have some debt to pay for the sins committed since we were re born into our Father's heavenly family. So the abuse we receive from our enemies, while visitors in this evil kingdom, is more rewarding than our afflictions. Such abuse will apply extra credit toward our payment at the 'day of judgment'. You are receiving your punishment now and being done with it now, so you don't have to pay off any unfinished debt at judgment. Therefore you should love your enemies and thank them for their help. They are your benefactors.

"At present, we are guests in this kingdom and must not consider any retaliation against our host because that would defeat our purpose. We are here to invite not fight, but when our Christ returns, God have mercy on this evil kingdom. At that time, our Lord will brutally deal with the unrighteous in our defense, crushing the evil king by force. First He came as a lamb, next time He will be the Lion!"

Peter was finished for the day so we rounded up the others and set off for our lodging. As we traveled my mother began talking and asked of me what become of my father. I said: "My father went in search of you, and the twins, Faustinus and Faustinianus, and that was the last anyone ever heard of him. Looking for you was the only choice he had in life. He was wasting away, tormented at the thought of never seeing you again. He must have died a long time ago, by shipwreck or heartbreak." She, hearing this only sighed, for her great joy on my account lightened her other sorrows. The next day she journeyed with us, accompanying Peter's wife. We came to Balaneae, where we stayed three days and then went on to Laodicea where Niceta and Aquila met us before the gates and escorted us to our lodging. But Peter, seeing that it was a large and splendid city, suggested we stay seven more days. After settling in our rooms my mother took a much needed emotional rest. Niceta asked me: "So, who is our new guest Peter has brought home this time?" I replied: "That is my mother that I have not seen in twenty years and was sure she had long ago died. Our wonderful God has reunited us by means of Peter."

Peter began to relate the whole matter to them in order: "I was asked to go to the neighboring island of Aradus to see the columns and art work. When we came to the place, we all went into the interior of the temple. When we came out, I felt compelled from my heart to visit the beggar women outside the door. I inquired of her, why she was begging and not working? She told me her whole story, how she was born of noble blood, as was her husband and had to leave Rome with her twin boys because of developing issues with her husband's brother; how all was lost at sea in a great storm, the ship breaking into many pieces, right under her feet. She was lifted by a wave upon a rock and day dawned and she spent the day searching. She never found any signs of her sons, Faustinus and Faustus. She has forever since been stricken with grief and just lingers on in life hoping to gain just enough courage to kill herself and end her...."

Peter stopped speaking, noticing Niceta and Aquila were both frozen and staring at the closed bedroom door, not listening to a word he was speaking. Breaking the silence, Niceta and Aquila both at the same time said: "This is impossible. This can't be!" Peter responded: "Impossible what?" Aquila, after a long pause, now both boys – eyes locked each other, said: "We are those twins you speak of! Faustinus and Faustus are our birth names and she is our...MOTHER!?"

Peter replied: "O' yes Clement, this is indeed a very interesting day the Lord has bestowed upon us." They immediately insisted on seeing their mother, but Peter stopped them, saying: "First, let me prepare her mind. She has already had enough emotional shock for one day, even though it was good. Right now she is getting greatly needed sleep."

When our mother had risen from her sleep, Peter began to address her, saying: "I wish you to know, O' woman, an observance of our religion. We worship one God, who made the world, and we keep His law, in which He commands us first of all to worship Him and to reverence His name. Then we must honor our parents and to preserve chastity and uprightness. But this also we observe: not to have a common table and eat with the gentiles unless they receive the Truth we speak of and truly believe it. Then after receiving the Truth they fast and are baptized, consecrated by a certain threefold invocation of the blessed name. Only then do we break bread with them. It is our belief that when we eat our meals, we consume the flesh and blood of our Lord and King. By our meals He resides inside of us, so only the true believer may participate. It could damage or even kill an unprepared person. (John 6:53, 1 Corinthians 11:30) Even if it were a father or a mother or wife or sons or brothers, we cannot eat at the same table with them until they are baptized. It is a part of our way. So do not be offended that you and your son cannot eat together until you, by free choice, accept our faith." [see Eucharist, page 241]

When she heard this, she said: "So let me be baptized today? Before we met, I had long abandoned those whom they call gods because they were not able to do anything for me, although I frequently and almost daily, sacrificed to them. And as to chastity, neither when I was rich nor when I was poor did I indulge in promiscuous pleasures."

My brothers hearing her speaking broke through and embraced and kissed her. She being startled and smothered uttered: "Stop! What is wrong with you two? Is this also a part of your faith?"

Then Peter said: "Woman, prepare yourself," after everyone settled down Peter continued: "these are your sons Faustinus and Faustus, they are now called Niceta and Aquila." Our mother, for what seemed the longest time, just looked at the boys. As she started to speak, she fainted. When our mother came to, she was calm and in total control of her mind and wanted to know all about the twins.

Faustinus began to speak: "On that very night, seconds before the ship went to pieces, a rogue wave out of the darkness ripped us off the deck of the ship as we were huddled together in a strong embrace. It happened so fast, we didn't even have time to think. When the wave left us, we were in the sea lying across the door we had been huddled against. Shortly after the break of day we were pulled from the sea by pirates, robbers of the seas. They took us to Caesarea and there tormented us with hunger and beat us and threatened us to never say a word. They gave us names and sold us at the market to a woman named Justa. She was a new convert to the Jewish religion and was wonderful to us. She adopted us as her own children and had us educated in the learning of the Greeks. Because of her, we became converts to the same religion and we have held steadfast to our One God and are well educated in all the other doctrines and philosophies.

"We also studied under the care of a Simon, a magician. At this time, stories began running through the world that a certain Man in Judea was saying: 'Those who have been pious are to live free from death and pain in His new kingdom,' which you will learn more about at a later time. Simon insisted we ignore the Man in Judea, but a friend of Peter's named Zacchæus warned us not to be led astray by the magician. Years later he introduced us to Peter so we could receive the truth and with time, we accepted 'The Way'. Therefore mother, we want to offer these same blessings to you so that we all may unite around the same table. Before we were dead at sea, but now we live. Beaten and starved by pirates, we were purchased by a wonderful pious woman and today our future is a blessed challenge."

When Faustinus had said this, our mother begged Peter to do whatever was needed, according to their faith, so she could fully be with her children and partake of food with them.

Peter responded: "If you truly believe, I will grant what you wish and in your case, your fasting time will be shortened because you requested that your hostess and benefactress should be baptized along with you. You would not have said such unless you knew that baptism was a great gift and for this reason I condemn many who, after being baptized and asserting that they have faith, do nothing worthy of the faith. Nor do they urge those whom they love, wives, children or friends, to become baptized. For if they had truly believed that God grants eternal life, they would urge those whom they loved to be baptized, instead of knowingly allowing them to live in sickness and in the end be destroyed. Where is the love in that? So, if they believed that eternal fire awaits others, they would not cease to rescue them. Since you have such confidence in baptism, you will fast for just one day instead of three."

She responded: "Actually, I have not eaten in two days. Only yesterday I took a little water. I have completely lost my appetite from all that has unfolded." Then Peter's wife, as a witness, confirmed what she said.

Peter smiling, replied: "But that is not a baptismal fast which has to take place on account of the baptism itself."

Faustinus interrupted: "Perhaps God, not wishing to separate our mother a single day from our table, has arranged her fast beforehand. Since she was chaste in the times of her ignorance, unaware she was doing what our religion required, perhaps God has arranged that she should fast just one day so she might take her meals along with us. After all, everything that has happened already must be divine providence."

Peter replied: "Our fasting is to repel the unclean spirits that attempt to control our bodily senses and not allow them to rule our inner senses, but to be in subjection to our inner senses, loving the things that are of God and not to follow the outer senses, which love the things that the flesh enjoys. As you sincerely desire, let your mother finish this day fasting and tomorrow she will be baptized and join us on our journey to paradise."

That same evening we all enjoyed the benefit of Peter's instruction' explaining how chastity is the commitment to just one spouse and none other, as our religion requires sole commitment and faith in one God. We are not to be dependent on government or money or lucky charms or superstitions or astrology or admiration of another human, for our lives and direction. That would be considered adultery against our Creator. Christ is the Groom, we are the bride. With our mother as an example, he showed us how the results of chastity are good, while those of adultery are disastrous and naturally bring destruction on the whole race. Disaster might be immediate or delayed, but either way, it will come as the result of adultery. Deeds of chastity please God so much that, in this life, He bestows some small favor on account of it, even for those who are living in error. Being faithful to one spouse is being faithful to one God only. For, salvation in the other world is granted only to those who have been baptized on account of their trust in Him and who also act chastely and righteously. Peter instructed: "This you yourselves have seen in the case of your mother where the results of chastity are in the end good. She would certainly have been cut off if she had committed adultery, but God took pity on her for having behaved correctly and rescued her from the destruction that threatened her and restored her lost children.

"But someone will say: 'How many have perished on account of chastity!' Yes; but it was because they did not perceive the danger. For the woman who perceives that she is in love with any one or is beloved by any one, should immediately shun all association with him as she would shun a blazing fire or a mad dog and this is exactly what your mother did, for she really loved chastity as a blessing, wherefore she was preserved and, as with you, shall obtain the full knowledge of the everlasting kingdom. The woman who wishes to be chaste ought to know that she is envied by wickedness and that because of the lust of many, caused by the evil king, they lie in wait for her. If then, she remain holy through a steadfast persistence in chastity, she will gain the victory over all temptations and be saved. Even if she were to do all that is right and yet should once commit the sin of adultery, she must be punished, so said our Lord.

"God, being one, created one woman for one man. The chaste woman takes pleasure in those who wish to be saved and is a pious example to the pious, for she is the model of a good life. She who wishes to be chaste cuts off all occasions for slander and if she be slandered herself by an enemy, she is blessed and avenged by God. The chaste woman longs for God, loves God, pleases God, glorifies God and to men she affords no occasion for slander. The chaste woman perfumes the Church with her good reputation and glorifies it by her piety. The chaste woman is adorned with the Son of God as with a bridegroom. She is clothed with holy light. Her beauty lies in a well-controlled soul and she is fragrant with ointment and a good reputation. She is radiant, for her mind has been brilliantly lighted. Onto a beautiful mirror does she look, for she is gazing upon God. Beautiful is the woman not because she has chains of gold, but because she has been set free from temporary lusts. The chaste woman is greatly desired by the great good King. She has been wooed, watched and loved by Him. The chaste woman does not furnish occasions for being desired, except by her own husband. The chaste woman is grieved when she is desired by another because she loves her husband from the heart, embraces, soothes and pleases him and acts the slave to him and is obedient to him in all things, except when she would be disobedient to God. For she who obeys God is without the aid of watchmen, chaste in soul and pure in body.

"Foolish is any husband, who discourages his wife from the fear of God. For who then will protect her from the influence and suggestions of the evil one? How will she remain chaste without a guardian of her soul?

"One adultery is as bad as many murders and even worse because it is not seen. When one is murdered, the dead body lies to be seen by all and displays a terrible vision of a brutal nature. But murders of the soul, by adultery are not seen by men and do not disturb the mind so much, yet the damage is more severe.

"Mattidia, you fled from the adulterer, that you might not defile the bed of your husband. People have suffered many evils on account of adultery, but you have suffered on account of chastity and thus were allowed to live. Had you died, your soul would have been saved just on account of your being chaste. Many trials people suffer are from the love of our Father. There are numerous benefits. It can build your character or change your life's direction for the good. Your experience in the sea was a baptism for the salvation of your soul. Your tribulation was all for the better. Had your children not been taken from you that night, they would have continued in ignorance and never known eternal life. And now you have them back, properly educated and prepared for the kingdom to come; by being deprived of your children for a little, they were saved for an eternity.

"Chastity is as powerful a tool as is baptism because it leads one to the door of baptism. It is so pleasing to God, that the chaste woman is God's choice, God's good pleasure, God's glory, God's child."

The sun had now concluded another wonderful day so we did our routine and turned to sleep.

"be strong in the Lord and in the strength of His might. Put on the full armor of God, so that you will be able to stand firm against the schemes of the devil. For our struggle is not against flesh and blood, but against the rulers, against the powers, against the world forces of this darkness, against the spiritual

forces of wickedness in the heavenly places. Therefore, take up the full armor of God, so that you will be able to resist in the evil day, and having done everything, to stand firm" (Ephesians 6)

Scroll VII

Much earlier than usual Peter awoke and woke us. Then he proceeded to direct us: "You three brothers come with me and we will take your mother down to the sea and baptize her while it is early, so we do not attract attention."

When we came to the sea, Peter baptized her between some rocks giving her privacy, since baptism had to be done completely nude - just as one is born of this world, breaking the water of the mother's womb and emerging unclothed. We brothers, along with some others, left because of the naked woman and we bathed elsewhere. Later we returned and took them with us to a secret place and prayed. Then Peter, on account of people gathering, sent all of us, along with our mother, back to our lodging. Peter came several hours after and breaking the bread for the Eucharist and putting salt upon it, he gave it first to our mother and after her, he gave it to us her sons. And thus we took food along with her and blessed God. "For everyone will be seasoned with fire and every sacrifice will be seasoned with salt."

Peter had us sit down beside him so he could explain why he sent us on before him after the baptism and why, he himself, was late in returning: "At the time that you came up an old man, a workman, entered along with you, who had been following us out of curiosity. When we came out he followed us and when I was alone, he took the opportunity to approach me and said: 'For a long time I have been following you and wishing to talk with you. I hear what you are telling the people and wanted to get you alone so I can tell you what I think. After you bathed in the sea, you went and hid and prayed. What a pity I felt for you because you are so led astray. There is no God nor is there providence, because all things are subject to fate. This I am assured because of the life that has been dealt me. I also am very educated in the sciences and they alone prove there is no creating and controlling God. Everything proven by our greatest minds of science shows all is happenchance. Whether you pray or not, you will endure the same fate that is assigned to you by genesis. Besides science, I am living proof that prayers are worthless, for they did nothing for me and don't let my ragged garments mislead you. I was once a very wealthy man of high social status. I sacrificed much to the gods, I gave liberally to the needy and yet, though I prayed constantly to my gods and acted piously, I was not able to escape my destiny.'

"I asked: 'What have you endured that has made you so bitter?'

"And he answered: 'I need not waste your time with my tormenting past. I can only save you the same pain and fully assure you that everything is subject to genesis. The planets and stars control all that happens in the lives of men and all human destiny. There is no single omnipresent, omnipotent God.'

"I responded: 'If you believe in your so called "genesis", why are you troubling me to change my ways when your own "genesis" belief would claim I am following my destiny? Therefore you cannot change me if you wanted to, prayers or no prayers. Your advice is contrary to your own opinion. For if man has no choice in his future, or has no "free will" and is destined to genesis, why would your soul be stressed with what I know is true for myself and if there is genesis, what or who created it?'

"While we were thus talking people gathered around us. So I said to all: 'I and my relatives have been handed down by our ancestors and our Lord the knowledge of the true God, Creator of all and we are commanded to give no heed to genesis or to science and astrology. For this reason I have no skill in astrology, so I will have to prove in another way that the affairs of this world are managed by divine providence and that each one will receive reward or punishment according to his actions, according to each one's own free choice. I can affirm that each one without doubt will reap the fruit of his deeds and I am proof alone, with the power given me by the great Creator, to cure any affliction man has thus voiding the theory of a destiny - controlling genesis. Your genesis offends God Who made all things because if all the evils of men and all their acts of impiety owe their origin to the stars and the stars are created by God the uncreated Creator, then you offend God by inferring His creation is evil and the sins of all are thus caused by God, Who is perfect. The truth is that man causes evil by his own choosing - errors in his free will.'

"The old man answered: 'I am still not convinced, because of my personal life. For I was an astrologer and dwelt first at Rome and then forming a friendship with one who was of the family of Caesar, I ascertained accurately the genesis of himself and his wife and tracing their history, I find all the deeds actually accomplished in exact accordance with their genesis and therefore I cannot yield to your argument. For my friend's wife, genesis was that which makes women commit adultery, fall in love with their own slaves and perish in the seas and her genesis came to pass. For she fell in love with her own slave and fled with him and perished in the sea.'

"I answered: 'How do you know for sure what happened to her if she was not around, and tell me more of this elite Roman person you speak of?'

"The man said: 'I am quite sure this is true because a brother of her husband told me the whole story of her passion. The brother was a very honorable man and the woman even tried to entice him to adultery, but he refused to pollute his brother's bed. She was thus a disgruntled woman and made up a dream in order to run off with a slave. She had no choice since she was adultery-obsessed because of her predestined genesis.'

"I inquired: 'What was this dream of hers you speak of?'

"'She said Juno, in a vision, ordered her to leave the city immediately with two of her children so her husband sent them to Athens for their education accompanied by servants, the husband keeping the third youngest son with him. He never heard from her again nor the children or servants and so unable to withstand the heartbreak, he devoted the rest of his life in a quest for them, giving up all he had in Rome to the youngest son. He soon after died a tormented heartbroken wretch of a man.'

"I, Peter, realized from what he said, the wretched man surely must have been Clement's father. So I asked him the names and he started to talk but nothing came out. Then, after a deep breath and a period of silence, he spoke softly: 'Faustus….' He said no more, then I replied: 'And Mattidia and Faustinus and Faustinianus.' He immediately moved as if to grab me: 'How do you know of them?' I quickly responded: 'I have heard of them…' Then he became aggressive and demanded on knowing how and where I knew of them.

"I told him: 'Calm down sir!' Then I continued: 'I am way late for my return and everyone is probably looking for me. After you regain your composure we can discuss this subject again tomorrow. For now, let me give you the place of... '

"He interrupted: 'I know where you stay.'

"So I promised him, again, that if he came by tomorrow we could discuss more.

"He replied: 'I will be there.'

"I turned and hurried on realizing everyone might be concerned as to my whereabouts, but I did not wish to disclose the matter to you before we had partaken of food, not knowing your reaction on this wonderful day of baptism when even angels rejoice."

After Peter told us this we were saddened yet very relieved to have closure on our father.

"Now let everyone...." Peter stopped speaking.

The old man was standing at the doorway. The room fell into silence as the man entered uninvited. When he looked on the woman he did not remove his eyes. Without any emotion he moved up to the woman and embraced her and they just stared at each other, not saying a word. Finally, our mother spoke: "Faustinianus is it really you? How are you alive?" When she said this I and my brothers immediately recognized our father as if a blinder had been removed from our eyes. Everyone was now speechless and not yet conscious of what was happening.

Peter, happily disturbed, said: "So, old man, why did you give me a fictions story?"

Our father still embracing and eyes locked on our mother did not respond. Finally, without taking his eyes off our mother he spoke: "Being of the family of Caesar, I did not want to be known. If I were recognized, the governor would send me back to Rome just to please Caesar. That is where they believe I belong, bestowing upon me that former prosperity I no longer had any use of, unless money could have ended my miserable life. I could never live like that, thinking I was the cause of death to those who were loved by me."

Peter said: "Were you also merely playing a part when you affirmed genesis?"

Our father turned his eyes to Peter still clutching our mother: "Sir I will not speak falsely to you anymore. I was in earnest when I maintained that Genesis existed. I associated with one who is the best of the astrologers, an Egyptian of the name of Annubion, who became my friend and disclosed to me the death of my wife and children."

Peter replied: "Are you not now convinced by facts, that the doctrine of Genesis has no firm foundation?"

He replied: "I know indeed, that astrologers make many mistakes, but frequently speak the truth and their mistakes are the result of ignorance because they cannot know all things with absolute accuracy."

And Peter answered: "You are O' so right my friend. Only a Prophet of the truth is always right."

The joy and emotions were beginning to overwhelm everyone in the room. We spent the whole night reuniting, as only Peter excused himself and turned to sleep.

"He will wipe away every tear from their eyes, and death shall be no more, neither shall there be mourning, nor crying, nor pain anymore, for the former things have passed away" (Revelation 21).

Scroll XIII

At break of day we all re-gathered with our mother, father and Peter. Peter addressing our father said: "I am anxious that you should become of the same mind as your wife and children so that you can all live together in the new kingdom and after the separation of your souls from your bodies you will all continue together free from sorrow. Does it not trouble you that you could lose them all again?"

And my father said: "I will never allow that bad choice again."

Peter said: "Then you had better diligently search your soul because at this time you are not headed to the paradise of your wife and children, but to a place of eternal punishments that will dwarf any pain and suffering you have experienced in this life from poor choices and if you wait too long and die, it will be too late. There will never be any chance of seeing them again."

The morning was moving along, so we all headed out to meet the people. Peter assumed his position and started speaking: "Clement, I would like your father to prove to you that nothing takes place outside of genesis and have you prove otherwise - that life and destiny are completely in our own control, by our God-given 'Free will' and that there are no other gods, planets, men or governments that can do anything about it."

I Clement, answered: "You taught that it is impossible for man to know anything of the truth, unless he learns it from the true Prophet.

"The will and purpose of God was to create a visible world for those few who would choose to be friends of His Son; people whom His Son can rule and have a wonderful relationship with. But the Father and the Son's consistency is of pure righteousness and good and it cannot co-exist with unrighteousness which we call evil or sin. Good and evil are pairs that define each other but also repel each other and can never coexist together. So that the Son can have good loving subjects, this present visible world was created to separate the good people from the bad ones and most everyone born is given a period of time to grow, in which they will choose 'good' or 'bad', by their own decision. The 'good' are those who follow the Ten Commandments, the ten rules given by the Father; the 'bad' are those who break the ten rules. Therefore the Ten Commandments become the controlling point of everyone's destiny [Ten Commandments page 257]. So the question becomes: 'how can a flawed man keep God's rules - from the outside by force or pain; the old covenant? Or from within, out of love for God and His will; the new covenant?" [Old and new covenant page 244]

"Then at an appointed time, only known by the Father, all the people who have ever lived, along with the ones still alive, will be harvested and sorted according to how they acknowledged the ten rules. Did they love and honor God. Did they treat their fellow men and women as themselves? We refer to that as the 'Day of Judgment'. After judgment, this present world will be destroyed and a new world will be birthed out of this old world, ten times more wonderful than this world we presently live in. It will be where our invisible heaven will become a visible world - a kingdom on earth as the kingdom now is in heaven. So, at this judgment day, all those souls who just believed in God and His Son will go to the new world to live with the new King, our

Teacher Christ. Some believers will first have to pay some unfinished debt, cleansed of any remnant sin, before going to the new kingdom, since God is 'just', fair and equal to all. At the same time, all those unbelievers who denied our heavenly Father will be destroyed by an eternal burning fire. So God has given us His rules, precepts, commandments and appointed a 'time'. He has promised a new world to come to those who chose to be members of His family. A visible kingdom on earth as His invisible kingdom now is in heaven. This new world will be for those who loved the Lord and a rewarding of their good deeds and for His Son to have loving good company that matches His consistency, which is pure goodness. People will be rewarded with treasures in the new kingdom in proportion to the good deeds they did for their fellow man while living in this evil temporary kingdom.

"This heavenly knowledge has been a hidden mystery to men who are full of themselves and is only allowed to be known by the humble. Man's knowledge of both arts and sciences was given by unclean spirits and can be learned and practiced by men - things learned from human instructors, not from the true Prophet. Father, you have gained your knowledge from human instructors and therefore believe in genesis, among other erroneous things, when in fact all mankind is controlled by the providence of God, along with our God-given 'free will'.

"Repeating again, God by His Son created the world as a double house separated by a firmament. Angelic powers dwell in the higher, called an invisible heaven and a multitude of souls born through women living lives in the visible, the present earth. From our world, He might choose loyal friends for His Son with whom He would enjoy fellowship, just as those of us prepared for Him as a beloved bride for a bridegroom, but even till the time of the marriage, which is in the world to come, He has appointed a certain power to select and watch over the good ones of those who are born in this world and to preserve them for His Son. Even with this protection 'free will' still must exist, so always be on guard for the prince of this world and of the present age is like an adulterer, who corrupts and violates the minds of men and seduces them from the love of the true bridegroom and lures them to strange lovers.

"But some will ask why it was necessary that an evil prince should be made, whose main purpose was to turn away the minds of men from the true prince? Because God wished to prepare friends for His Son and did not want them so by force, such as by necessity of nature they could not have been anything else. He wanted them so by their own 'free will' to choose good and to love His Son by their own choice. Therefore the providence of God has willed that many men should be born in this world, so that those who should choose a good life might be selected from many. He gave men freedom of mind to do as they please and pursue their desires, but they are all made with different talents and desires. Therefore the evil prince is the result of bad choices in man's free will.

"All men in this world could not be kings or princes or lords. There also had to be teachers, lawyers, mathematicians, goldsmiths, bakers, rich men, farmers, fishermen and even poor men. This was necessary for men to interact and be dependent on each other in order that by this interaction it would be determined which are good and worthy and which will be cast away, depending on how they treated each other as they strived to survive in this present world. Were they just selfish for themselves or were they giving and helpful to others? Inequality is necessary in this world, for there cannot be a king unless he has subjects to rule over. There cannot be a doctor unless there are sick or a fisherman unless there are hungry people.

"The Creator, knowing that no one would take up these professions nor would they work by choice, had to motivate man to do so. No one would come to the contest of his own because work and labor would have been avoided. Therefore, God made for men a body susceptible of hunger, thirst and cold, in order that they would participate in the contest, interacting with each other, whereby sorting out the good from the bad. For we, out of survival must cultivate every one of these arts for the sake of food, drink, clothing and shelter. So will a man supply the demands of hunger and cold by means of thefts, murders, perjuries and other crimes of that sort, or will he survive keeping the rules of God, using the labor of his hands to supply his bodily wants with justice, piety, mercy and also supplying the needs of others? If he is a victor in the contest set before him and is chosen as a friend of the Son of God then he wins indescribable trophies and treasures, but if he breaks the rules of the contest by carnal lusts, frauds, iniquities and crimes, he becomes a friend of the prince of this world and of all demons, the ones that taught him his actions and our Christ does not know him. He takes no self-responsibility but blames the bad hand your 'genesis' has dealt on some thing or some other person instead of the errors of his own bad choices. So in truth, he chose this path by his own free will. Professions are learned for the selfish desire for food, clothing, shelter and personal pleasures, but these selfish obsessions become weaker as one gains more and more knowledge of the truth and then the desire for excesses starts to subside. What reward will I get for all my hard labor to gratify myself, during these few years I live? Nothing, only good deeds done to other men can you take with you to the new kingdom to exchange for great rewards that last for eternity.

"At the end of this age, we will be judged. Did we act justly with him whom we paid wages for his work? Do we act mercifully to him in sickness or him in poverty, forgiving to those who cannot pay their debts? Did we maintain gentleness towards all, doing all things according to the rules of God?

"Therefore, if any person yield to impiety rather than resist it, he gives harbor to these unclean spirits within himself, degenerating into unrighteousness, with no self-control, rebellious against any authority and eventually allowing the unclean spirits to torment the body with afflictions and diseases. These demons can only encourage and incite, but cannot compel or accomplish.

"If any one give in to them and does those things the demon wickedly desires, he will be open to destruction and the worst kind of death. So do not turn into action what is conceived in evil thought.

"You might ask: 'I have so fallen for these deceptions in my mind, can I ever be saved?' Yes!! Just humbly ask and you will receive. Believe in our Christ and hurry to be baptized and you will be cleansed of all your past as if it never existed and your name is written into the book of life, but for the future, you must control yourself and beat back those evil desires or pay a debt in this life or after this life before entering the new kingdom. This can be done by reminding yourself of the reward that is waiting and also of the severe punishment that is waiting. And you also have a 'Helper' available, if you sincerely ask in prayer.

"But you ask: 'If any one fall into love, how will he be able to contain himself, even if he sees before him the fires of hell? For love can overpower the strength of a man or woman.' Then I tell you: pray for the strength of the Holy Spirit and by all means stay way clear of such persons of desire. You have their demon and your demon doubled up against your weak resistance to the flesh. If you are nowhere close to the person yours nor their unclean spirit can do anything. Any contact with them will be destruction of your own choosing. Leave Rome and move to Athens if you have to. If you allow any contact, you brought it on yourself. Demons can only strongly persuade, they cannot act!

"The astrologers, being ignorant of such mysteries, think that things happen to man by the courses of the planets and suns and this deceives many people because they become the authors of error. Unclean spirits are anxious to confirm the error of astrology because it makes it much easier to deceive, when no one knows it is actually demons manipulating man's mind.

"Many people have committed murder, adultery and other horrible crimes and have not seemingly physically or mentally suffered from the unclean spirits. Such are people who practice wickedness hurting others who have done them no harm and are the same people who have no intention whatsoever of repenting. For these people God defers their punishment to the future age. The evil prince needs them healthy to continue doing his bidding; as the devil said: 'You work for me and I will give you anything in my kingdom for your pleasure.' People with evil minds do not deserve to be punished and corrected in this present life. The evil is so imbedded that any punishment in this life would be a waste of time because it could only be temporary and of no consequence.

They have no love for God or their fellow man. God only punishes in this life those He loves, His children, for their own good correction. So many unrighteous are allowed to occupy this present life as they wish. When they finally die in this life, their actions will have demanded the extreme punishment of eternal fire in hell and finally their souls will scream for repentance, but it is way too late and they will never find peace. Therefore praise the Lord for your afflictions. Since we all sin, it shows we have a loving caring Father and if you do not suffer in this evil kingdom, you might need to do some deep soul searching.

"do not take lightly the Lord's discipline,
and do not lose heart when you are being disciplined,
because the Lord disciplines the one he loves,
and he chastens everyone he accepts as his son or daughter.
Endure hardship as discipline; God is treating you as his
children. For what children are not disciplined by their father?
If you are not disciplined, and everyone undergoes discipline,
then you are not legitimate, nor true sons and daughters at all."
(Hebrews 12)

"Each one of us, who sins, with his own free will chooses
punishment, and the blame lies with him who chooses. God is
without blame " (Clement of Alexandria).

"Fear of Hell is a great tool for repressing undesirable lusts because who are there among men who do not covet their neighbor's goods? And yet they are restrained and act honestly, through fear of the punishment prescribed by the government laws. Through fear nations are subject to their kings, kings being just simple single men and the king's armies obey him, even though they are the ones holding the weapons of destruction. Slaves, although they are stronger than their masters, through fear, submit to their masters' rule. Even wild beasts are tamed by fear. The strongest bulls submit and huge elephants obey their masters. Also unclean spirits are put to flight by fear. The fear of God restrains everything and keeps all things in proper harmony and fixed order and you may be assured that the lusts of unclean spirits which arise in your hearts may be completely abolished by God's counsel and warning - the fear of God."

Then our father replied: "Clement you have wisely spoken and remind me of myself. Every country or kingdom has laws imposed by men that no one easily transgresses without incurring a punishment."

And I, Clement, responded: "These different laws and customs are so imbedded in the people it makes it hard to spread God's truth, which is very different from man's truth. This is the challenging adventure we enjoy, as we move through the different peoples of the world.

"The Seres, in east Asia, who dwell at the beginning of the world, have laws like the Jews, not to kill or commit adultery, not to use prostitutes or steal and not to worship idols, but different from the Jews, in all of their country which is very large, there is neither temple, nor image, nor harlot, nor adulteress, nor is any thief brought to trial, neither is any man ever slain there and no man's liberty of will is compelled. Among the Seres the fear of laws is very powerful. They are a mild and healthy people living over 120 years and it is a land of much silk and their country produces everything in abundance. They are tall with blue eyes and make strange sounds when they talk, but they are a compassionate people, living in comfort, peace and harmony.

"Then there are the Bactrians in India. They are peaceful, committing neither murder nor adultery. They do not have idols nor do they eat animals and they do not get drunk and always fear God. But the rest of the Indians commit murders and adulteries. They worship idols and are usually drunk and do all kinds of wickedness. In one part of India, if strangers are caught, they are butchered and eaten.

"The Persians marry mothers, sisters and daughters.

"With the Geli, women cultivate the fields, build and do all the men's work and are allowed to have intercourse with anyone they would like and their husbands do not care. They have promiscuous intercourse everywhere and especially with strangers and they do not use ointments or wear dyed garments or shoes.

"The men of the Gelones are adorned, combed, clothed in colored garments with gold and other metals, but they are not feminine; they are very warlike and good hunters.

"In Susae, the women use ointments and ornaments and precious stones. They travel a lot with maidservants while the men stay home and they have intercourse with whomever they please, slaves and guests. Their husbands do not care and the women also rule over the husband.

"In a remote part of the East, if a boy is sexually molested and it is discovered, he is killed by brothers or parents and left dead and un buried.

"The Gauls allow boys to be molested publicly and there is no disgrace.

"In certain parts of Britain several men have one wife and the British will copulate in open public.

"In Parthia many women will share a husband. Every part of the world has its own rules and customs.

"The Amazon women have no husbands or men. Like animals, they go out from their own territories once a year and live with the men next door and when they have conceived, they return home. If they birth male children, they dispose of them.

"The Medes throw men to dogs to be eaten alive.

"The Indians burn their dead and the wives voluntarily are burned with them.

"So now, today, the Romans have brought everyone they have conquered under their law and civil decree.

"Barely seven years have passed since the righteous Son of God was with us. People from all nations came to Judea to see Him and His miracles and learn His doctrine. Then they took it back to their own countries where they rejected the old lawlessness and their incestuous marriages.

"Thomas (doubting Thomas), who is now preaching the gospel to the Parthians, writes to us saying that many have now given up polygamy.

"We are told the Medes no longer throw their dead to the dogs. The Persians stopped having intercourse with mothers and daughters. The Susae women are being faithful to their husbands.

"So it is obvious fate and genesis could not control the lives and actions of men, or they could not change of their own will. Man relies on the fear of laws and God's judgment to come, to resist all our desires and curtail the violence of sinning.

"Our minds are subject to errors in two ways: Things passed down to us from customs we call the commandments of men; second is the natural lust in men which hostile demonic powers feed on and encourage us to do. Both can be checked by the knowledge of truth, the Love of our Creator and the fear of impending judgment"

Niceta breaks in: "Father, you, like us were raised under the knowledge of man, not God, and the philosophers whom we all studied were of the opinion that the body was made out of matter consisting of four elements of which there is a coming together of many into one. These elements come from a simple atom that cannot be dissolved like the body. Therefore we believe the body was made into its shape using combinations of these diverse simple matters by One whom we call God, the Creator of the world and the One we acknowledge as author of the universe. We do not believe the complicated world we see could have come together by random happenchance or fate. For it is evidently the work of mind and reason, with a direction.

"Who, having even a particle of sense, sees a fabulous house with all its purposes for comfort and shelter custom made just for man, cooking, bedrooms, bathrooms, library, gathering room, would pronounce it was created accidently by winds and debris over millions of years?

"Who can be so foolish and blind as to look up into the heavens, see the splendor of the sun and moon, the beauty of the stars, all fixed by laws and periods and not recognize a wise and rational Creator, wisdom and reason itself?

"The divine providence allows us to admire it, but places in secret the way in which it was done so it will be unknown to the unworthy, but may be disclosed to the worthy and faithful."

Father replied: "I am impressed! You boys are indeed wise. Providence could not be better described, but as it is now late, I wish to continue this discussion tomorrow." Then we all rose up and returned to our lodging, took dinner and went to sleep.

"Do not put faith in every spirit, but test the spirits to discover whether they proceed from God; for many false prophets have gone forth into the world...every spirit which acknowledges and confesses that Jesus Christ has become man and has come in the flesh is of God....He Who lives inside of you is greater than he who is in the world...God sent His Son, the only begotten, into the world so that we might live through Him...not that we loved God, but that He loved us and sent His Son to be the atoning sacrifice for our sins....No man has at any time seen God. But if we love one another, God lives inside of us and His love is brought to completion in us...By this we come to recognize that we live in Him and He lives inside of us: because He has given to us of His Holy Spirit....In this communion with Him love is brought to completion and attains perfection with us, that we may have confidence for the day of judgment because as He is, so are we in this world." (1 John 4)

Scroll XIV

On the following day Peter got up early and called us. We went to where we were on the previous day and prayed and afterwards he said: "Everyone according to your own God-given ability needs to work to spread the faith. Do not hesitate from instructing the ignorant in everything you have heard from me and I from the Teacher. Do not speak anything which is your own, though you may think it to be true. Only speak what you have heard from me - no more, no less. It will come that people will wander from the truth because at times, through unclean spirits suggestions to their own thoughts, they think they have discovered a truth more powerful. Man's thoughts get tangled and corrupted from all the mind influence the evil one has, as most of your thoughts are not your own."

Then Peter said: "Aquila, you may start today's discussion."

Aquila responded: "There are two visible signs shown in heaven: the sun and the moon. There are also five other stars each describing its own separate orbit. God has made and placed these in order to give us temperature and seasons. These therefore, God has placed in the heaven by which the temperature of the air may be regulated according to the seasons so that we have a variety of weather. Also, they are used by God to send plagues and disasters upon the earth, when man's sins require such action. By this, order can be kept or destroyed. From these heavenly bodies 'time' is also created. God also uses the sun's activity to produce ice ages and heat cycles. The moon is used for the growing of crops and animals and all living things and by its waxing and waning everything born is nourished and grows. Therefore, when the will of God deems it necessary, He can change the steadfast order of His planets and suns so that chastisement may come upon men for their errors.

"You ask: 'why would God bring chastisement upon both the pious and the impious?' It is because of what Peter said before about afflictions and receiving abuse from your enemies. Chastisement is to the advantage of the pious, where being afflicted in this present life they will become more purified for the future life in which eternal treasures are prepared for them. Also, during chastisement, the righteous give thanks to God, while the unrighteous blaspheme and curse the Creator - the Creator they will not even acknowledge! They curse the God they claim does not even exist. Those who have learned the truth know for what reason blight, hail, pestilence and the like, have occurred in every generation and for what sins these have been sent as a punishment where sadness and grief resulted, all because some have abandoned and disrespected their Creator.

"In the beginning of the world there was none of these evils, but they took their rise from the impiety of men and as iniquities increased, evils also increased. So for that reason divine providence decreed a judgment for all men, pious and impious, because everyone could not be dealt with according to his deserving. Yet there have been some nations that rejected evil, like the Seres and because they live chastely and no one there eats unclean flesh, or knows anything of sacrifices, they are kept free from plagues, living to old ages and die without sickness. But we, miserable as we are, dwelling with wicked men, get to suffer with them the plagues of afflictions in this world. This is the reason Moses had such strict laws, such as the death sentence for breaking any commandment. He did not want to suffer for the errors of stubborn other people with whom he was forced to live with."

Their father replied: "You would think God would not punish the righteous with the unrighteous, but would have a way to spare the righteous."

"God," said Aquila: "Did. He cleaned the earth of the unrighteous with a flood saving the one and only righteous man left on earth, Noah. The flood, you call Deucalion. After the flood, the descendants of Noah slowly sank back into unrighteousness because the flood of punishment had faded from their memories and eventually was erased from the records of their history. Since God would not use a flood again, He selectively cleaned the earth with His own people when they retook Canaan under Aaron's command, then later conquering more peoples with the judges and kings. At the same time, He granted that certain angels who enjoy evil could have power over certain individual men, but under strict conditions - only if that individual transgressed God's commandments! These evil-loving angels, we refer to as 'demons' or 'unclean spirits'. They are the souls of the human-angel crossbreeds whose bodies were wiped from the earth by the great flood and are not allowed back into heaven. So they prowl the minds of men, looking for victims through which to continue enjoying their evil pleasures through men's bodies - men they convince to sin. When man first sinned, he gave birth to evil - the down side of 'free will'. Yet 'free will cannot exist without 'evil' because one would have no choice and there would only be 'good' to choose from. Every good thing has a corresponding contrary evil thing joined with it. We call it 'contrary pairs'. As cold is to hot, hurricane is to sea breeze, destructive animals to gentle animals, such is good to bad. As there are pious men, so there are also impious prophets and false prophets, magic arts to angels of God, demons to the Divine, Christ to the devil. So which of the pairs directs your life? Worship of gods created things such as money, planets, men and governments, or the worship of God the Creator?

"The same applies to 'order' and 'disorder'. All are the result of the creative all-powerful direction of God we call 'order'. Then there is 'disorder'. Given enough time, life and everything else will appear out of nothing and evolve into highly sophisticated compounds and this is an error in thinking caused by ignorance.

"If a large boulder fell from a mountain and burst into billions of pieces, would one fragment emerge in the perfect figure of your goddess Venus?"

Our father answered: "That would be impossible."

Aquila, responded: "What if there were a stone mason present at the mountain and his hands and his mind could form anything he would like?"

Our father answered: "What is your point?"

Aquila replied: "If there is not a rational mind, no figure can be formed, but with a designing mind, there can be both form and chaos. In like manner, the things which are done in the world are done by the providence of a contriver, even though they sometimes seem disorderly.

"There is also the pair of belief and unbelief, so one must flee from unbelief before it leads him to the prince who delights in evil. Therefore follow the way of faith that brings one to the King who delights in good men and women."

Father said: "You have stated it excellently, my son."

Aquila continued: "All men should desire knowing what is best for them. Therefore they should seek after the true Prophet, for He alone knows all things and knows what every man is seeking. He is within the mind of every one of us who has invited Him in, but for those who have no desire of the knowledge of God and His righteousness, He is not in their minds or bodies. So seek Him first of all because you will not learn anything from any other. He is easily found by those who diligently seek Him through love of the truth and patience and whose souls are not in the control of the wicked one. He deserts those minds wishing to do evil and as a Prophet, He knows the thoughts of everyone. Let no one think he can find Him by his own wisdom, unless he empty his mind of all wickedness and has a pure and faithful motive to know Him.

"Consider this work of divine providence. The philosophers have introduced difficult words so that not even the terms that they use can be known and understood by all. They are arrogant and self-centered and use complex words to make them appear intelligent.

"From their arrogance, God has kept them ignorant of His knowledge. It is only given to the humble and modest - who enjoy simple, plain and brief words. So the self-important people are kept in darkness by the Creator and they will never be allowed to know right or wrong, black or white, cold or hot. They will only be lukewarm. For arrogant men can never come to any truth of knowledge and learning and their lives stay filled with uncertainty. Therefore they will find the end of their lives sooner than the end of their questions. For this reason God does not want to be known by the unbelieving. As the blind arrogant would say: 'If God is there, why will He not show Himself?' He did seven years ago and these men are as blinded by God now as they were then.

"Father, you must not think yourself like Caesar or the philosophers. You must humble yourself and recognize your life is on the wrong path. Ask for help and forgiveness. Then and only then will your eyes be opened and understanding enter your mind."

Peter spoke: "Just look at your past and you will see divine direction. It was God's will and love that separated your family from you for your family's own salvation. For, if they had remained with you, they would have never known the truth of life. So it was arranged that your children should travel with their mother, should be shipwrecked, thought to have perished and should be sold. The boys would be educated in the learning of the Greeks, so that having knowledge they could better refute the Greek doctrines. They united with me to help with my preaching; Clement should join us to help financially and to record the Word. Then your wife was found and saved and now here we stand, all reunited in Gods time line. You now stand before two paths that will direct the outcome for the rest of your life and eternity. One path leads to destruction, the other path to an eternal paradise so wonderful man's simple mind cannot comprehend.

"Suppose that there were two kings, enemies to each other, having their kingdoms cut off from each other by 'time'. The first king has sovereignty over the present kingdom, the 'time' we live in now, where a law from heaven has been imposed. This king can rule over and punish all subjects that break the heavenly laws, but the good people also living in his kingdom, the keepers of God's laws, he cannot touch because they have deserted and belong to the good King, the future kingdom to come at a future 'time'. The subjects of both kingdoms are separated and sorted by 'free will'. Those who choose the present have power to be rich, to revel in luxury, to indulge in impious pleasures and to do whatever they like, for they will possess none of the future goods. But those who have determined to accept the blessings of the future reign have no right to the things that belong to the present evil king's kingdom except food, clothing and shelter, all gained by the work of their hands, for we are considered temporary unwanted visitors of a foreign kingdom. Plus, the 'good' will receive additional goodness and abundance overflowing, as God delights and decides to bestow."

The day passed quickly. Night had arrived, so we partook of food and went to sleep.

"If you love me, obey my commandments. And I will ask the Father, and he will give you another Advocate, who will never leave you. He is the Holy Spirit, who leads into all truth. The world cannot receive him, because it isn't looking for him and doesn't recognize him. But you know him, because he lives with you now and later will be inside of you (Eucharist)" (John 14).

Scroll XV

At break of day Peter went out and reaching the place where he was to speak, found a large crowd already assembled. Before he started speaking, Simon himself walked up, along with two companions.

Simon spoke first: "So, I hear you have found Faustus and really think you can convince him, a wise man, that there is only one God if any at all. I have come so you may not deceive such an intelligent man with your simple man's doctrine." Then turning to our father: "Tell me most excellent of all men, is this man trying to prove to you that there is only one God and whoever acts contrary to His will would suffer some kind of eternal punishment?"

Then addressing Peter, Simon said: "Your own scripture says when Adam and Eve ate of the tree of the knowledge of good and evil, God said: 'Behold, Adam has become as one of us,' inferring God has many other equals because the serpent said: 'You shall be as gods.' Your scripture also states: 'You shall not revile the gods, nor curse the rulers of your people,' and: 'Let the gods that have not made the heavens and the earth perish.' Also: 'Take heed to yourself lest you go and serve other gods whom your fathers knew not.'"

And Peter said: "There is only one great God; everything else is subordinate and a creation of His. 'The Lord your God is God of gods', also: 'As I live, says the Lord, there is no other God but me. I am the first and the last; except for me, there is no God.'"

Peter continued: "Simon, the statue they made of you is no god. It is made of stone and cannot see, or hear, nor do anything. Yet we still refer to it as Simon's god, instead of Simon's piece of rock. So, it is God's way of communicating with the misled minds of men who think these creations are gods. Man creates many gods through the error of his mind - objects man thinks can lead and protect him through this life. When in truth, there is only One Who can guide and protect. Even Moses became a god to Pharaoh, though in reality he was just a man. The same is the case also with the idols of the gentiles, but we have one God only, who made creation and arranged the universe, whose uncreated begotten Son, is the Christ."

And Simon said: "Your scripture says: 'and God said, Let us make man in our image, after our likeness.' Now, 'let us make,' implies two or more; certainly not one only."

And Peter answered: "God is three identities, the Father, the Son and the Holy Ghost, all of which are one. A tree we consider as one, yet it has a root, trunk and limbs; then leaves and fruit. Starting with the root, the rest of the tree is an extension. The root of the tree controls while the rest of the tree springs forth from the root. Therefore the root would represent God; the trunk and limbs are our Teacher and King, Christ; the fruit of the tree would be considered the Holy Spirit - three separate, but the one same tree. Man's body is one, yet it has multiple parts that do the will of the mind. The mind says to the hands: 'stretch out and create.' It says to the mouth: 'speak forth my words, thoughts and will.' God said to His Wisdom: 'Let us make a man.' But His Wisdom was that with Whom He Himself always rejoiced as with His own spirit, God united as one, yet extended out, as a hand, creating the universe, just as your hand is a 'hand' of itself yet is united to you as part of the body as a whole. Also, one man was made and from him a female went forth. So God Himself looks upon man and wife as one: 'A man shall leave his father and mother and be joined to his wife and the two shall become one flesh.' Man and wife are two, but to God they are one. Therefore I offer up the honor to One God as if Parents.

"We call Him God whose peculiar attributes cannot belong to the nature of any other. He is boundless, where everything else is contained within bounds. How great is the mercy of God and his forgiveness to them that turn to him. God is so great and incomprehensible, that when man has done all he can to find out His greatness and boundless perfections, he has just begun to learn, for what he has found out is but a mere nothing in comparison with God's infinity."

And Simon said: "Do you really believe that the image of man has been molded after the image of God?"

"I am certain, Simon."

And Simon replied: "Then how can death decompose so great an image?"

Peter explained: "It is the shape of the just God. Man's body representing God must remain good, but when the body begins to act unjustly, such body can no longer represent a perfect God. Therefore the body is dissolved back into the earth from which it was created. But all bodies that ever lived and were dissolved will be recreated in order that there can be a judgment of the good deeds and the bad deeds and each man rewarded or punished accordingly, in the same body in which they originally did the deeds. Then the ones who loved the Lord will finish any unpaid judgment debt and will be changed into new eternal bodies and sent to the new kingdom. The unbelievers will join you, Simon, in a place of eternal torment."

Simon said: "Why would such a great God make His image, man, out of dirt?"

Peter answered: "This was done because of the love of God, who made man. For, man is composed of all elements of God's creation - the earth and the universe and all the elements of creation have been made for the service of man. Man absorbs parts of all creation as he grows into his shape. Through the food that man eats, he grows into the form of the Creator, made from the atoms of the creation itself and through consumption of food also come unclean spirits. Upon death of the body, man returns what he used to its original owner: the earth. These substances willingly endure man, who is inferior to them, just to honor God because of our image, just as man honors a statue of the Emperor made of rock whose shape the rock just happens to have. This gives honor to the Emperor himself even though it is just a rock. So the whole creation rejoices in joy serving man, just because of man's shape, not his substance.

"Simon, you are obsessed with persuading us to be ungrateful to our Creator and yet you still stand. God is boundless and long suffering to bear with as great an impiety as yours and not already have dissolved you. But our Teacher said; 'Many will come'. So if not you, your prince would find another useful ignorant from a pool of many. Simon, you commit spiritual adultery, which is worse than the carnal. For, it was God the Creator of heaven and earth who in former times punished sins when He was blasphemed in the highest degree and would inflict the severest punishment, but now, He is long suffering, waiting on repentance. But the time will come when He shall sit down to give judgment to all who ever lived. Therefore let us fear the just God whose shape the body of man bears for honor."

Simon answered: "Enough of your ignorance and insults for one day. I will return tomorrow." And after Simon said this, he went out.

Peter then said to everyone present: "Yes indeed, this is just the start. For there will be many yet to come and much to test the people - false apostles, false prophets, heresies, governments of man, money schemes and desires for supremacy - all false, deceiving doctrines of man, disguised as truth, finding their beginning in Simon."

Then Peter laid his hands on people and prayed after which he dismissed all until tomorrow and we did our usual and went to sleep.

"whatever you desire that others would do to and for you, then so do also to and for them, for this sums up the Law ...for wide is the gate and broad is the way that leads to destruction, for many ...But the gate is narrow and compressed that leads to life, and few will find it....Beware of false prophets, who come to you dressed as sheep, but inside they are devouring wolves....Every tree that does not bear good fruit is cut down and cast into the fire. Therefore, you will fully know them by their fruits....Not everyone who says to Me, Lord, Lord, will enter the kingdom of heaven, only he who does the will (commandments) of My Father Who is in heaven....Many will say to Me on judgment day, Lord, Lord, have we not prophesied in Your name and driven out

demons in Your name and done many mighty works in Your name? (but we didn't keep Your commandments)...And then I will say to them, I never knew you; depart from Me, you who act wickedly and disregarded My commandments. " (Matthew 7:12)

Scroll XVI

The next morning, after sunrise, I Clement, Niceta and Aquila, along with Peter, came to the apartment in which my father and mother were sleeping and finding them still asleep we sat down on the steps before the door. Peter said: "Listen, I know that you have a great affection for your father; therefore I am concerned that you will urge him too soon to take up our religion while he is not yet prepared for it and of course he would consent, through his affection for you.

"This cannot be depended on. For what is done for the sake of men will not last and soon falls to pieces. You cannot force or entice someone to change. You must allow his 'free will' to work and he has to fully accept in his own heart and mind. The truth has to come from within. Your father needs time to hear and learn the truth first. Therefore it seems to me that you should permit him to live for a year according to his own judgment and during that time he may travel with us and while we are instructing others he can hear and learn. Then at any time, of his own choosing, he may take up the yoke of our faith. If not, he will always be a friend. For those who do not take it up heartily, with their faith strongly rooted in them, can easily be diverted and deceived. Being young in the faith, they are still too ignorant of the truth and since the unclean spirits attack the believers much stronger than unbelievers, their early faith can easily be tested. If the new recruit stumbles, the devil can easily persuade him that he is unworthy of God's grace. As the going gets harder by the trials and attacks of these unclean spirits, they despair by the excuse of their weakness and reject and speak evil of the truth. They can become worse than before, even evil in nature.

They become spiteful and critical in manner against us. So they need time to become strong against these deceptive voices so they have the whole knowledge of truth to rebuke them. You would never send an untrained solider into the heart of the battle. He would quickly feel unworthy of his King and surrender to the enemy."

Niceta answered: "What if my father should die within the year during which you recommend that he should be put off in order to confirm our faith? He will go down to Hell helpless and so be tormented forever."

Peter replied: "God judges fairly the hearts of men. If anyone has lived righteously, he shall immediately be saved. He will be examined by Him who knows the secrets of men as to how he has lived, whether according to the rule of the gentiles, obeying their laws. For those who have lived righteously without knowing God, for the sake of God alone and His righteousness, they shall come to eternal rest and shall be brought into the new heavenly kingdom. For salvation is attained by faith in God. Also, God knows events before they take place and knows whether this man is one of His.

"When I speak to you with your father present, ask a question about matters for him to learn and while we speak to one another, he will become educated. Wait first to see if he himself will ask anything and we will go from there. If he doesn't, then we will take turns asking each other questions."

Then I, Clement, suggested to Peter: "Because my father thinks you fully know all things on this matter, which indeed you do, be sure you don't present a question as though you needed enlightenment. So it might be best if my brothers and I discuss the knowledge, then you can interrupt and correct us."

To this Peter answered: "Let us not concern ourselves about this since God is in control of all things. If indeed it is fitting that your father decides to enter the gate of life, God will afford a fitting opportunity and there shall be a beginning from God and not from man. And therefore, as I have said, let him journey with us and hear our discussions." While we were thus talking, a boy came to tell us that our father was now awake and on his way.

Our father came out and said: "There is a saying very prevalent among the Greek philosophers to the effect that there is, in reality, neither good nor evil in the life of man. 'Good', being whatever produces the best consequences upon the lives of people, especially with regard to their states of well-being. 'Do unto others as you would have done unto you'; and evil is hurting other people and animals, done with pleasure and satisfaction, for unclean spirits that feed on the pain and suffering of mankind, just waiting for any excuse to pounce. But some men call things good or evil by their own personal definition, depending on the use and custom of life. For, not even murder is really an evil, because it sets the soul free from the bonds of the flesh. Neither do they say that adultery is an evil, for if the husband does not know, or does not care, then where is the evil in it? No one is hurt. They were done unto like they would have done. So, adultery can be good. Neither is theft an evil, for it takes away from those who have and gives to those who have not. For all men ought to have the common use of all things that are in this world, with no personal ownership, since everything belongs to God. In short, a certain man, the wisest among the Greeks, knowing that these things are so, says that friends should have all things in common and that includes wives. He also says that, as the air and the sunshine cannot be divided, so neither should anything else. All of which we are given in this world, should be possessed in common."

Peter answered: "Actually that wise man you quoted is describing the new kingdom to come, but in this present kingdom, sharing everything in common will never work, because of the 'evil' created by mans 'free will'. Go tell Caesar that he should share everything he has in common. Man's sinful selfish nature will not share anything in this evil kingdom. Jealousy and envy are the reason wars arise, cities are destroyed and countries fall. There will always be those who will strive to take from others, until Christ returns. As long as evil is alive, men will always strive and scheme to take from others, particularly under the disguise of 'in common', or by any means or doctrines that justifies men's selfish lustful needs.

"Self-important wise men take many things from what they read and create an opinion of truth. Therefore great care is to be taken that when the law of God is read, you do not read and comprehend it according to the understanding of our own mind. Half and distorted truths have been taught and learned by man, always. For you must read it just exactly as it says and discard your whole life's learning. Clear your minds and believe and take the sense of truth from the Scriptures themselves and not from man's opinion of what they should say because man will manipulate the scriptures until it says what he wants to hear, disregarding the truth. Man resists being convicted (Repentance). So they water down the 'Truth', making it lukewarm.

"...They will follow their own desires and will look for teachers who will tell them whatever they want to hear." (2Timothy 4:3)

"God has created us so that all minds are conscious of Him and He rejoices if any one, on hearing the preaching of the truth, does not delay or hesitate, but immediately detesting the past (Repents), starts to desire things of the future and is eager to enter the heavenly kingdom.

"Do not procrastinate, for why delay to do well? Do you think when you have done well you will not find the reward as you supposed? And what would be your loss if you do well without reward?

"He gave to men holy baptism and if anyone comes quickly and for the remainder of his life works his best to remain pious and without stain, all his sins are blotted out which were committed in the time of his ignorance. This is a sign one sincerely believes in his rebirth because they will henceforth diligently strive to follow the Lords commandments: 'If you love Me, you will keep my commandments'. As I explained before, it is like your marriage. If one says he loves his spouse and commits adulteries, he never really loved his spouse in the first place. Our Teacher went to the cross for us out of love and if we do not have enough love for him to overpower the love for our desires, after the torture He went through for us, then we never loved in the first place and our sins were never forgiven because we never truly believed (Hebrews 10:26). The King will not continue receiving the grotesque punishment due for those who do not really care about Him. Those who are not sincere with true love inside their hearts are only displayers on the outside to impress other men and women instead of God. Your actions speak more than words:

'We are not trying to please people but God, who tests our hearts.' So yes, all your previous sins in ignorance are forgiven and erased from the book of record and will never be brought up at judgment, if you truly love the Lord. But one must show his love by obeying his loved One. Otherwise forgiveness never happens and payment will be due in full on judgment day. Also, with the Eucharist, Christ will be in you and the Holy Spirit can help one fight the demon influence, but only if one asks and truly desires help."

Peter continued: "Philosophers know only the present and visible, but we speak of things man cannot know on his own. Man has no way of determining invisible things or the origin of the world, the end of the world, the judgment, and new world to come. This truth, only by first believing, comes from prophetic knowledge alone - things of the past, future and things invisible; invisible, in that our Creator did not give us that detector, as in a nose to smell, ears to hear, eyes to see, skin to feel. It can be detected inside only by faith in prophetic truth, as this doctrine of ours is. Once a true believer, your heart will confirm its presence. This is why one wonders why others do not feel it also? The reason they do not feel it is because they do not believe in Christ. Belief will give the desire, never felt before, to know and learn more of this new love of your Creator and so great a sweetness and peace it will be."

After Peter had spoken, he cured some present who were possessed of unclean spirits, which had been causing them sickness and injury. Peter then invited them to come to the same place on the following days for the sake of hearing the true message. Then he dismissed the crowds giving thanks and praising God.

We all then retired to our lodging to take food and sleep.

"I love those who love me, and those who seek me find me.

With me are riches and honor, enduring wealth and prosperity.

My fruit is better than fine gold; what I yield surpasses choice silver.

I walk in the way of righteousness, along the paths of justice, bestowing a rich inheritance on those who love me and making their treasuries full" (Proverbs 8).

Scroll XVII

The next day Peter was to hold another discussion with Simon. So he rose earlier than usual and prayed. Then Zacchæus came in and said: "Simon is here, talking with about thirty of his own special followers."

And Peter said: "Let him talk until all have arrived."

Zacchæus came back later and said: "He accuses you Peter of being the servant of wickedness, of having great power in magic and of charming the souls of men in a way worse than idolatry."

Peter finished praying and went out and standing in the place where he spoke the day before, he began to speak: "Our Lord Jesus Christ, who is the true Prophet, made concise statements regarding the truth having only a limited time assigned Him for teaching. He just stated the facts and did not spend any time in arguments with men uninterested in learning. He spent most of His time personally educating us for our missions to come. If we did not fully understand what we were told, He would patiently go over and over, until we all thoroughly understood.

"We were well prepared to take it into the known world and we were told to teach people the first of His commandments: 'Fear the Lord God, and serve Him only.' Then, secondly, tell the people to honor God's image, man. Like us, He has every limb and body part but only for beauty, not for use. He does not have the same eyes that we need for our visual world. He sees without eyes, in all directions and His body is so brilliant, eyes like ours could not withstand His light. He is more splendid than anything

He created, so that in comparison with Him the light of the sun is darkness. Nor has He ears, for He hears, perceives, moves, energizes, acts on every side, but man does have the same shape as His most beautiful shape, so that God's creation will honor man and man can be the ruler and lord of all. Man is the visible image of the invisible universal Creator. Therefore, if man desires to worship God, he will honor other men. What any one does to man, be it good or bad, is regarded as being done to God. Therefore judgment hinges on that, giving to every one according to his merits, considering how he treated his fellow man. For God avenges His own shape.

"God, who truly exists and reigns in a superior shape, sends forth the power and energy to propel the entire universe. He is the heart of all and He is a substance infinite in height, boundless in depth, immeasurable in breadth, creator of life, wise over all infinites. He is the heart and center of infinity proceeding out to everything and being the limit of the universe who Himself possesses a figure.

"God has seven extensions outward. First are six temporal intervals that completed the world and universe: height above, depth below, to the right and left, to the front and back. The seventh Himself, His true image, will be the new age and world to come, the Kingdom of Christ. For in Him the six infinites end and from Him they receive their extension to infinity, as the period of seven days equals a week. The seventh day is a day of 'rest'. Therefore, God himself will be the 'rest' for all who qualify for the new kingdom. He, the seventh, completes the whole."

Simon then responded: "You claim that you have a better understanding of your Teacher because you saw His deeds with your own eyes and heard Him speak with your own ears and that it is not possible to know Him by apparition, visions or ghosts."

And Peter said: "You think one who hears or sees through an apparition knows more than one who personally lived with him and that you therefore know more than I of the truth? The Teacher allowed all our senses to behold Him - our sight, our touch, our ears. Therefore, we could believe with confidence, as (doubting) Thomas would confirm, being examined and questioned as the disciple wishes, but anyone who trusts in an apparition, vision or dream is sure to be insecure, for he cannot be certain of what he saw because demons as deceptive spirits do this all the time. An unclean spirit knows everything about anyone who ever lived and can easily imitate him, pretending to be what it is not and saying whatever it likes. The demon can appear and disappear just like its king, the evil one."

And Simon said; "You claim that apparitions do not always reveal the truth, in visions and dreams, even if sent from God?"

And Peter replied: "How can you understand an apparition, if you cannot even understand me? Again, you have no idea if what you are seeing is from God, or if it is an unclean spirit in disguise, which happens more often. One is always uncertain of apparitions and who needs a vision to learn and know what he ought to do?"

Simon responded: "Let us dismiss this subject."

"Not so fast," said Peter: "You started it, I will finish. I know for a fact, you could not have seen Christ. His light is so intense your human body would have perished. Our new convert Paul was blinded just by a close encounter. Had he looked upon Christ, it would have killed his body. God cannot be seen by man who lives in flesh because he who sees God cannot live. Only if flesh is changed into light like the angels, so that it can see light or light be changed into flesh, so that it can be seen by flesh. For, the light would dissolve the flesh of him who sees. The power to see the Father, without undergoing any change, belongs to the Son alone.

"Just for the believers, after the resurrection of the dead and the judgment and payment in our old bodies, we will be changed into light and become like angels. Then we will finally be able to see our Creator. And also, whenever an angel is sent to man, it first has to be changed into flesh in order to be viewed by man's eyes. If one sees an apparition and not a man in flesh, he can be most assured that this is the apparition of an evil demon.

"On the other hand, you can hear the voice of God whether awake or in sleep and you can have visions of symbols or representations. You can have it just enter your mind, as when I pronounced our Teacher the Son of the living God. That type of knowledge is learned without instruction, apparition or dream.

"What appeared to you Simon was a demon. If our Teacher appeared to you in a vision and made Himself known to you and spoke to you, why are you so violently against me, who was a close companion and student of His? A house divided will not stand. I am of one kingdom, you of another."

Simon replied: "This is enough of your babble for today." And as usual, without nod or goodbye, Simon turned and left.

With Simons leaving, we ended the day as usual.

"God is compassionate and merciful, and will forgive sins in the day of tribulation: and He is a protector to all that seek him in truth. They that fear the Lord will be able to keep His word: and they that love Him, will keep His way and His commandments, and will have patience until His return." (Ecclesiasticus)

Scroll XVIII

At the break of day when Peter headed out, Simon was already there and said: "I have come to show you that He who framed the world is not the highest God, but that the highest God is another who is also good and who has remained unknown up to this time."

Peter replied: "Simon, believe whatever you wish. That is the point of 'free will'. For you can only know and understand the One and only God if you are worthy and the Son reveals Him to you.

"Tell me Simon, do you maintain that the Son, whoever you believe He is, is just, or that he is not just?"

And Simon said: "I believe that he is most just."

Peter said: "Seeing He is just, why does He not make the revelation to all, but only to those to whom He wishes?"

And Simon said: "Because being just, He wishes to make the revelation only to the worthy."

And Peter: "Must He then know the mind of each one in order that He may make the revelation to the worthy?"

And Simon said: "Of course he must."

Peter said: "He alone knows the mind of every one and obviously, the truth has not been given to you, who cannot even understand what I am telling you."

When Peter said this, the people applauded.

Simon irritated said: "I maintain that there is some unrevealed power unknown to all, even to the Creator himself, as Jesus himself has also declared, though he did not know what he said. For when one talks a great deal he sometimes hits the truth, not knowing what he is saying. I am referring to the statement which he uttered, 'No one knows the Father.'"

"Do not any longer profess that you know His doctrines," said Peter.

Simon said: "I do not profess to believe his doctrines, but I am discussing points in which he was by accident right."

And Peter said: "Simon, you believe there were two angels sent forth, the one to create the world, the other to give the law. Neither one of them proclaimed: 'I am the sole creator', or that there is one who stands. You believe that there is an unrevealed power who is full of ignorance since it did not foreknow the rebellion of the angels who were sent by it to monitor man's activities."

Simon said: "It is not proper to reveal to the people secret doctrines. They are not worthy to know."

And Peter said: "I will not allow them to get trapped into false doctrine, just because they are ignorant of the truth."

Simon said: "You are evidently not able to reply."

And Peter: "No one knows the Father but the Son, nor does anyone know the Son but the Father and they to whom the Son may wish to reveal Him. I am amazed that you would think the statement is made in reference to the ignorance of the Creator (Demiurge to Simon) and all who are under him. You claim Christ was the son of David and not the Son of God. The reason you are confused is, as I have said, that the Son will not reveal Himself to unbelievers. He gives that revelation to whom He wishes. He gave the knowledge to Adam, Enoch, Noah, Abraham, Isaac, Jacob and Moses. This revelation has all along been given only to the people who were worthy. We were taught not to get frustrated at those who cannot understand, because God has a block on their minds. They are intentionally blinded to the truth.

"It is now possible for all to know Him through His Son Jesus. 'I have concealed these things from the wise, and have revealed them to sucking babes.'

"Aren't you, Simon, the standing one, who has the boldness to make these statements which never have been made before?"

Simon said: "Blame your own Teacher."

Peter responded: "The way that leads to the kingdom, is the way of living your life. Does one follow God's Commandants as he goes through life? When one asked Him: 'What shall I do to inherit eternal life?' He pointed out to him the commandments of God. We are followers of 'The Way'. Our Teacher said: 'I am the way and the truth and the life. No one comes to the Father except through me.'"

Simon changed the subject: "So, Peter, since you say there is an 'evil one', explain how a just, righteous and loving God would create and allow evil.

Peter responded: "God created man with free will, then man by his God-given choice, created evil. God is not the author of sin. If man had not sinned and disobeyed God, man's body would not have died or been afflicted. Placed before every man is life and death, good and evil and that for which he chooses will be given to him. If man were sinless, the poison of snakes would have no effect. Neither could poisonous plants have an effect on man, nor could unclean spirits disrupt the body. By sinning man became capable of every suffering including death. All this evil, this suffering, we created all by ourselves on account of our voluntary choice. If man had never disobeyed his Father, evil would have never existed."

And Simon replied: "He made the angels a different composition from man, but gave them the same 'free will' and some of them rebelled against God, being disobedient also. Their leader, the wicked one, departed from a state of righteousness. So, why has God honored the wicked one with a post of command? Is it not plain God is sponsoring evil?"

And Peter said: "He could not have chosen a better subject. The archangel Lucifer disobeyed the laws of angels and was cast from heaven. Since God cannot be a part of unrighteousness, there was the perfect one for the job: evil angels ruling over evil men. The devil gets to rule over those who are just like him and he even gets his own evil kingdom. His job is to inflict punishment on those who sin, a temporary position until judgment day. The wicked ruled by the wicked one, with sinners being punished by him with sickness and afflictions."

Peter added: "But Simon, you are the evil king's ambassador and have no desire to learn anything from me. Your whole intention is to disprove God and lead people to eternal destruction. You are obsessed with proving God does not exist, thinking judgment would then go away. Our Lord and Teacher commanded us: 'Keep these mysteries for me and the sons of my house'. He told us all these mysteries of the kingdom of heaven privately and said not to waste them on those who only want to argue and dispute and have no intention of learning: 'Do not give what is holy to dogs and do not throw your pearls before swine, or they will trample them under their feet and turn and tear you to pieces'. I participate in these discussions so the people can utilize their 'free will', having before them the good and the bad.

"So evil comes from man's error, usually out of ignorance, producing pain and death and death is nothing but the separation of the soul from the body. At which point the body, incapable of sensation, is dissolved and the soul, which has sensation, continues to exist and remain in existence and the righteous soul becomes immortal, entering the peaceful reign of Christ. Then the soul will have no irrational impulses and its knowledge will be unerring, so it will know evil from good and pain will be no more."

And Simon said: "But what about man's emotions - lust, greed, anger, and such?"

Peter said: "Lust was put into man so there would be an attraction to the other sex and people would populate the earth. Then there will be a select few, out of many, that will be fit for eternal life. If it were not for lust, no one would trouble himself with intercourse with his wife. Gratifying himself for pleasure, he carries out God's will and using lust for lawful marriage, he is pious. Using it like an irrational animal, he becomes impious and is punished, because he makes bad use of a good thing. Anger was given us for communication, correction and self-defense, but if used unrestricted, it is impious. Grief makes us human, giving us the ability to have sympathy and affections for others.

"There is also a long forgotten code of proper times that will cause man afflictions, besides the afflictions of unclean spirits caused by sins. Because men follow their own pleasure in all things, they started cohabiting without observing the proper times to do so. The egg being fertilized at the wrong times brought on a multitude of evils. God fixed seasons for planting and sowing and so also He made seasons for cohabitation, which should have been carefully observed. That is why Moses called them sons of the new moons and the Sabbaths. Since man today is ignorant of this, children have been born with innumerable afflictions. The correct seasons are given by Enoch, who received the instructions from God. Since we only knew afflictions were caused by sin through demons, we asked our Teacher what sin did a certain man or his parents commit for him to be born blind? Our Teacher answered; 'Neither did he sin at all, nor his parents, but that the power of God might be made manifest through him in healing the sins of ignorance.' Such afflictions arise because of ignorance, not knowing when one ought to cohabit with his wife if she be pure from her discharge: 'There is an appointed time for everything and there is a time for every event under heaven, a time to give birth and a time to die; a time to plant and a time to uproot what is planted.'

"The main reason for our afflictions are our sins. It is because of the love of our heavenly Father we receive correction: 'Those who spare the rod hate their children, but those who love them are careful to discipline them.'

"But along with ignorance of proper times, there are three more reasons for afflictions.

"The first is the case of Job. The devil told God that the only reason Job loved God was because He gave Job anything he wanted. If life for Job went bad, Job would hate God. In other words, God was paying Job off, for his love. Job held steadfast to God no matter what the tribulation and in the end, he was repaid double for his trouble.

"The second is so we will interact with each other. Getting sick or afflicted brings in the services of a doctor, nursing and other occupations. The interactions test us, how we will react to God and with others. Will our behavior be good or bad? Also, there cannot be a doctor unless there are sick or a fisherman unless there are hungry people.

"The third is the case of Clement. If Clement and his family had not gone through tribulations, the whole family would have been lost to eternal hell. Their afflictions, unknown by them at the time, resulted in their salvation. As I refer to the problems in a believers life as being for some unknown good; first the bad then the good; contrary pairs."

Simon said: "Speaking of doctors and hungry people, does not the inequality among men seem to you most unjust? For one is born poor, another is rich, one is sick, another is in good health."

Peter said: "Simon, we were talking about evil; however, there could not be pious or righteous people, unless there were also needy people for them to help."

And Simon responded: "Then those in humble circumstances are cursed by God because they are distressed so that others may be made righteous."

Peter answered: "If their humiliation were eternal, their misfortune would be very great, but in this temporary kingdom the fortunate and unfortunate take place according to lot and he who is not pleased with his lot can appeal, by pleading his case before God, to exchange his mode of life for another."

And Simon said: "What do you mean by this lot and this appeal?"

And Peter continued: "Being born again and changing your direction in life and living according to the law of God, you will obtain present blessings along with eternal salvation. But you must truly believe, pray and ask and have faith and patience knowing God will change your circumstances. If one loses the faith he loses the blessings."

Simon responded: "I have listened to you speak on all these topics and am not convinced of any of this."

When Simon said this and was on the point of leaving in his usual way, my father said: "Listen to me Simon. Having heard you both discuss in turn, I realize that Peter is the one speaking the truth. You have nothing to say of benefit, only to argue. You Simon have been defeated."

And Simon, hearing this, went away in silence, but Peter stayed for the rest of the day laying his hands on the large assembly of people, healing all that needed. Then Peter retired to the house and sat down with the rest of us.

Sophonias said: "Praise the Lord O' Peter, who selected you and instructed you for the comfort and salvation of everyone willing. You presented the truth to Simon with great patience and you must be worn out, having to discuss with such an obnoxious, arrogant man."

And Peter said: "On the contrary, if you do what you love, you will never work a day in your life."

So we all partook of the evening meal and went to sleep.

"For we ourselves also were sometimes foolish, disobedient, deceived, serving various lusts and pleasures, living in malice and envy, hateful, and hating one another. But after that the kindness and love of God our Saviour towards man appeared, by the washing of regeneration, and renewing of the Holy Ghost, which He shed upon us richly, we became such as we are. For God sent forth His Word and healed them, and delivered them from their destructions," (Orgen 200AD)

"If you remain in me and my words remain in you, ask whatever you wish, and it will be done for you. This is to my Father's glory, that you bear much fruit, showing yourselves to be my disciples" (John 15).

Scroll XIX

In the nighttime Peter got up and woke us, and then sat down and said: "Ask me questions about anything you like." And Sophonias was the first to begin: "I know you have already explained several times, but will you explain to us again what the real truth is in regard to evil?" Peter said: "Yes, I have explained it many times but it is necessary by fellowship with each other, to revisit these truths over and over lest the evil one will confuse you and snatch it from your mind, just as the Lord's commandments must be constantly stamped in your minds and hearts for your own well-being."

Then Peter retells: "God appointed two kingdoms and established two ages, determining that the present world should be given to the evil one because it is small and passes quickly away, but He promised to preserve for the good people the age to come, as it will be great and eternal. Man, therefore, He created with 'free will', giving him the choice to do anything he wanted. Man's soul has two sets of three parts of passions. The first is the female part: lust, anger and grief. The second is the male part: reasoning, knowledge and fear. All these result in the actions of man. Now, two ways or two paths have been laid out before all people: the path of obedience to the commandments of God and the path of disobedience. And also two kingdoms have been established: the one called the kingdom of heaven to come, and the other, the kingdom of those who are subjects of the present kingdom. Also two kings have been appointed, of whom one (devil) is selected to rule by law over the present and temporary world. This king rejoices in the destruction of the wicked. But the other, the Good one (Christ), who is the King of the age to come, loves the whole nature of man, but is not able to have any rule in the present world. Yet He is allowed to counsel what is advantageous to the subjects of this present kingdom, like One who is a spy or guest in an enemy kingdom

"But of these two, the one acts violently towards the other by the command of God. All men have it in their 'free will' to obey whichever of them they please by the doing of good or evil. If any man chooses to do what is good, he becomes the possession of the future good King. But if anyone should do evil, he becomes the servant of the present evil one, who has received power over such man by just judgment on account of the man's sins. Wishing to use this power before the coming new age, he rejoices in punishing man in the present life. Thus by gratifying his own private passion, he accomplishes the will of God.

"The good King rejoices when He finds a righteous man and saves him with eternal life. Now it is within the power of every unrighteous man to change and be saved and all previous sins are pardoned. But from then on, every righteous man may have to undergo punishment for sins committed after he was saved. These two leaders are the swift hands of God and are here to accomplish His will. 'I will kill, and I will make alive; I will strike, and I will heal.' For, in truth, He kills and makes alive.

"God kills through the left hand, the evil one, which has been so composed as to rejoice in afflicting the impious and He saves and blesses through the right hand - that is, through the Good one, His only begotten Son, who rejoices in the good deeds and salvation of the righteous. The wicked one, having served God blamelessly to the end of the present world, can become good by a change in his composition, since man's ability to make errors in his choices will come to an end."

Micah asked: "What then is the reason why men sin?"

And Peter said: "It is because they are pleasure seekers, originating from the two sets of three passions each. And not all pleasures are good. For in consequence of their ignorance, as I said before, they are urged on through fearlessness and unclean spirits to satisfy their lust through evil pleasures in an unlawful manner. Therefore God is not evil, who put lust within man so that life will continue, but man is evil who uses a good thing incorrectly. The same applies to anger."

Lazarus said: "Explain how the evil one, the punisher of the impious, will be sent into lower darkness along with his angels and with sinners. I remember that the Teacher Himself said this."

Peter answered: "The evil one does no evil, inasmuch as he is accomplishing the law given to him. Man does evil and although he did rebel against God and has an evil disposition, through fear of God he does nothing unjust except accusing the teachers of truth so as to entrap the unwary, giving him the title of the 'accuser'.

"As our Teacher said, the evil one and his angels along with the sinners shall go into lower darkness. The evil one rejoices in darkness and delights in going down to Tartarus along with angels who are his followers. For the composition of Hell is the same as his and he and his angels love it there, but the composition of the souls of men are different and cannot withstand the atmosphere of Hell. So the souls of men, not capable of dying are extremely tormented there, until they pay the debt of unrighteous while they lived in the present kingdom.

"Once all deserving souls are in Hell, some for short terms, others for eternity, evil will have come to an end and the devil will no longer be evil since evil will no longer exist because there will be no men left to give it cause. At such time the devil's composition will then be changed to good. At the beginning he feared God and only did God's will - sorting good men from bad and punishing evil men.

Joseph asked: "Why, when you speak the truth to a group of people, do some believe and others disbelieve?"

And Peter answered: "There again, it is 'free will'. Some are fertile ground, some are not. My discourses are not charms, so that everyone who hears them must without hesitation believe them. The fact that some believe and others do not, points out the freedom of 'will', which has been given to all. There are the stubborn hard hearts and there are the fertile hearts of the variety of men. When you plant seeds, some produce abundantly, some average and some nothing at all and just drain life support from the other plants."

Everyone was now hungry, so we got up to go get food. Then someone entered and said: "Appion has just come with Annubion from Antioch and they are lodging with Simon."

My father hearing this, said to Peter: "Please excuse me sir. I would like to go and say hello to an old childhood friend."

And Peter said: "Surely, that is a good gesture."

After we ate, we stayed up that whole night listening to Peter speak on many subjects. So engrossed were we in what he was telling us, we didn't even realize it was daybreak. Peter stopped speaking and looking at my brothers, said: "I wonder what has become of your father?" And while he was speaking my father came in. When he had saluted he began to apologize for being gone so long, but we, looking at him, were horrified, for we saw on him the face of Simon, yet we heard the voice of our father and when we backed away from him, my father was astonished at our reaction. Yet Peter was the only one who saw his natural countenance and he asked us what the problem was?

We, along with our mother, answered him: "He appears to us to be Simon, though he has our father's voice."

Then Peter replied: "I can still see his face, but from what you say, Simon must be into his sorceries." And looking at my father he said: "Sir, it appears Simon has placed his face on you."

While we were standing there in confusion, a messenger entered and said: "Simon is now in Antioch and is inciting the people to hatred against you, calling you a magician, a sorcerer and a murderer. We fear, if you go there, harm might come against you.

"While our group was there in Antioch trying to figure out what to do, there came Cornelius a centurion of Rome, sent by Caesar to the president of Caesarea on public business. We explained to him what was happening and asked if he could help us. He said: 'What a coincidence! Caesar has ordered me to gather up sorcerers and bring them to Rome to be destroyed. Many magicians have already been rounded up from the provinces and killed.' But when Simon learned Caesar was hunting for him, he fled the city and we believe he has come back here."

So Peter could not go to Antioch until the hatred Simon had produced had lessened. Peter, looking at our father said: "Faustinianus, your face has been transformed by Simon Magus because he was being sought by Caesar for punishment. He placed his own countenance upon you, so you might be apprehended instead of him and put to death."

My father said: "Why would he? I have done Simon no harm."

Anubion came in and said: "Simon has left here and headed for Judea." Looking at our father we were all amazed and still confused. Peter said: "Believe me, this is your father and I insist you treat him as such. For there is an unknown good that will result from this and God will correct this silliness of Simons and your fathers face will be restored."

Anubion said: "When we met with Simon he asked us to invite Faustinianus to come over and eat at our table with us. With Faustinianus partaking of food, Simon would have the power over him to work his magic. Simon told us he was doing this to get even with the sons of Faustinianus for abandoning him and joining with Peter. I am still able to see the true countenance of your father because I was previously anointed by Simon himself so that the real face of Faustinianus might appear to my eyes. I must say, I am a bit impressed. It evidently worked since all of you do not recognize your father."

Peter broke in: "We will first use Simon's trick to our advantage and then I will restore your fathers face. Leave Clement with me and go on ahead of us to Antioch with your wife and your sons

Faustus and Faustinus. I shall also send others with you for assistance.

"When you get to Antioch you will be thought to be Simon. Stand in a public place and proclaim your repentance and disclose: 'I, Simon, declare to you and confess that all that I said concerning Peter was false. For, he is neither a seducer, nor a magician, nor a murderer, nor any of the things that I spoke against him. I said all these things because I am a confused man. I now know Peter is truly sent by God for the salvation of the world, a disciple and apostle of the true Prophet. You should hear him and believe him when he preaches to you the truth. Since I am deceptive with many personalities, if I ever come to you again telling lies about Peter, ignore them. In fact, it is I myself who is a magician, a seducer, a deceiver.'"

When Peter gave this plan to my father, my father replied: "This will be fun and entertaining - Simon bit by his own deception."

And Peter said to inform him when the people have calmed down and he will come into the town: "At that point I will free you from Simons face."

As we were about to leave, our mother refused to come, nauseated at the thought that she might have to sleep with Simon, but Anubion promised to keep them separate until his face was restored - she reluctantly agreed and we all left for Antioch.

While Peter was daily teaching to the people and working many miracles and cures, a messenger arrived informing Peter that the plan had finally worked, but at one point almost backfired: "Faustinianus was doing such a good job, the people wanted to destroy him for the damage he had done to you. We were able to rescue him but the anger might rekindle. It would be best if you hurry there to restore his face." Peter replied: "Consider it already done, my friend."

That evening Faustinianus had his own face restored to him and the appearance of Simon Magus left him, without Peter even being present. When Simon returned to Antioch, he received a surprise welcome. The people spat on him and drove him from the city, warning him if he ever tried to return, he would be responsible for his own death.

Before Peter left for Antioch, he ordained a bishop and presbyters and baptized multitudes and restored to health all who were troubled with sicknesses and unclean spirits. He stayed there three days longer until all things were settled and put in order. Then we all said farewell to the city.

The whole city of Antioch heard Peter was coming and set out to greet him. Old men and the nobles came with ashes sprinkled on their heads, in this way testifying of their repentance for believing the magician over Peter. The people brought to Peter their sick, their demon-tormented and paralytics. The people showed great faith in God and believed that all who suffered from every sort of ailment could be healed by him. Peter spread out his hands towards heaven and gave thanks to God, saying: "I bless you, O Father, worthy of all praise, Who fulfills every word and promise through Your Son, that every creature may know that You alone are God in heaven and on earth."

Peter had them bring all the sick before him and told them: "I, myself, am nothing but a mere man just like yourselves, who can do nothing to help you. But He who came down from heaven, for only those who believe in him, is the perfect medicine for body and soul. With your whole heart and being, let it be known that you believe in the Lord Jesus Christ, Son of the only God, our heavenly Father." All the people declared with one voice: "He is the true God whom Peter preaches." Suddenly an overpowering light of the grace of God appeared in the midst of the people and the paralytics began to run to Peter, the blind were shouting on the recovery of their sight, the sick were rejoicing. Even those being barely alive or unconscious regained their health.

So great was the Holy Spirit on that day that all from the least to the greatest with one voice confessed the Lord. Within seven days more than ten thousand men and women, believing in God, were baptized. Theophilus, a wealthy man, even gave his palace to be used as a church and a chair was placed in it for Peter. The people assembled daily to hear Peter speak the words from God.

Then I, Clement, with my brothers and our mother spoke to our father, asking him if he was still a stubborn unbeliever. He replied: "Let us all go see Peter." When Faustinianus approached Peter he said: "Sir, the seeds of your word which were planted in the field of my mind have sprouted and matured. My mind is now ready to be separated from the weeds by that spiritual reaping hook of yours. You may place me in the care of the Lord, making me partaker of the divine table, the body and blood of your Lord, King and Savior." Then Peter, grabbing his hand, presented him to us saying: "Just as God has restored your mother to her sons, your father has also come home." Peter proclaimed a fast to all the people and on the next "Lord's day" he baptized Faustinianus in the midst of the people. Peter ordered the people to meet on the following day and having ordained one of his followers as bishop and others as presbyters, he baptized a great number of people and restored to health all the lost souls who had been distressed with sicknesses.

In the year of our Lord 39AD

The next day the soldiers departed, our mission just beginning; traveling through enemy territory inviting all slaves to abandon their evil king and his impious ways and become family of the Good King, the Son of God. Keeping His commandments and entering the eternal kingdom to come.

In the year of our Lord 2011

Christianity is the largest religion, two billion+, one third of the world population, with thirty-seven thousand+ denominations.

Conclusion

What became of Simon the magician

(From the Acts of Peter)

When Peter finally made it to Rome, the people brought on the Sabbath, many of their sick, those who suffered every kind of affliction of the body. Peter healed any who believed in the name of Jesus Christ and very many were added every day unto the grace of the Lord - God's mercy, just by faith alone, given to the undeserving - relieving them of eternal punishment.

Simon the magician was telling the people that Peter was a deceiver. His God was not the true God and when Simon did many deceptive wonders, they who were firm in the faith and knew the truth, mocked and ridiculed him. Simon would make spirits that were not real appear in his dining room. He made some lame men walk and some blind to see, but for those he professed to heal, their recovery only lasted a short time. The demons would obey Simon briefly, but never leave the afflicted persons. Peter followed him throughout and convicted him always before everyone. So the people of Rome treated Simon with contempt and disbelieved him, since he never succeeded in doing the things which he promised to perform. Simon, being in such a plight at last said to people: "You think Peter has prevailed over me as more powerful and so you pay more heed to him. I tell you, Peter has deceived you, but since you receive his words over mine, cursed be to you all. Even though I have become weak, I shall fly up unto god whose power I am. Since I am the standing one, I shall return back to my father."

The next day a great number of people gathered to see Simon fly away and Peter joined the assembly, so he could bring the son of the evil one down once and for all. When Simon had entered Rome ahead of Peter, he deceived many with his flying illusion.

So when Simon, standing on a high place saw Peter, he said: "Peter, today as I rise to the heaven, all the people will know who I am."

When Simon started rising up above Rome, the faithful to the Lord looked at Peter in confusion and Peter, seeing the illusion spoke to Christ saying: "Lord Jesus Christ, if you allow this magician to deceive in this manner, all the faithful will be lost again. Please hasten Your grace and bring the evil one down." Thus so it happened and Simon fell from the sky and broke his leg in three places. Then every man cast stones at him and from that day forward, everyone believed Peter.

One of the friends of Simon who had given him much money came to his aid. He saw that Simon had severely broken his leg and said: "O' Simon, what happened to the power of your god? You are broken to pieces. You are a fool and a fake." The man then left Simon lying there in torment and followed after Peter.

Simon finally found someone to carry him by night, on a bed, from Rome to Aricia, where he lay there broken for a long time. They finally found another sorcerer to operate on him, but Simon died during the surgery. Thus, Simon the angel of Satan finally came to his end.

What became of Peter

Peter stayed in Rome rejoicing in the Lord with the believers and giving thanks night and day for all the people who were brought daily unto the holy name by the grace of the Lord. Among those who converted and believed, were the four concubines (girlfriends, mistresses) of Agrippa the prefect. Once the girls learned that the Lord required chastity, they realized they had a huge problem, but because of the love of the Lord and His commandments, they all agreed to remain chaste. As you can imagine, Agrippa became very annoyed and frustrated. One woman could never satisfy his pleasure demon. It didn't take long for Agrippa to discover the source of his growing irritation and he became furious and told the girls he would destroy them and burn Peter alive if they did not return to his bed.

At the same time, a very beautiful girl belonging to a friend of Caesar was converted and became chaste.

Many other women also, loving the word of chastity, separated themselves from their husbands' girlfriends. They desired to worship God in sobriety and cleanness and the one wife - one husband rule started running throughout Rome.

The Roman elite gathered and made it clear to the authorities the same would happen to them if they did not take action, even though chastity broke no known Roman law. So, they all agreed to create a fictitious violation against Peter. They accused Peter, with many sexually frustrated false witnesses, of being a dealer in sorcery.

Peter was informed of the plot against him and encouraged to leave Rome in haste.

Peter responded: "Should I run from the truth?"

And they said: "No, but you must be preserved in order to continue the Lord's work, saving so many people. You are worth so much more alive than dead." So, Peter accepted their advice and left Rome alone. As he was on his way outside of Rome, Christ appeared to him heading into Rome.

Peter said: "My Lord, where are You going?"

The Lord said to him: "I go into Rome to be crucified."

And Peter said: "Lord, crucified again?"

The Lord said: "Yes, crucified again. Peter, I am very proud of you as I knew I would be. Your work is finished and it is now time for you to come home."

Then after Peter watched the Lord ascending back up into heaven, he pulled himself together and returned to Rome rejoicing and glorifying the Lord, saying: "I am being crucified."

He went back to the believers and told them about the visit from our Lord. Peter said: "Do not be troubled because if it is the Lord's will it will come to pass, no matter how much we try to resist it and run from it, but for all of you, the Lord will strengthen you in his faith and send you abroad in my place so that you also may continue the battle and bring others to Him. But the Lord has finally called me to come home to Him. It will be the most wonderful day of my entire existence. I will have finished the race and my labor will be over and rest and paradise will welcome me forever."

While Peter was speaking four soldiers arrived and took him away. When they brought Peter before Agrippa the prefect, Agrippa commanded Peter to be crucified on an accusation of godlessness. Peter said nothing and was pleased at the thought.

All the believers gathered together in order to rescue Peter - rich and poor, orphans and widows, weak and strong. They rioted and would not be silenced, shouting: "What wrong has Peter done, Agrippa? How have you been hurt? Tell the Romans!" And others said: "We greatly fear if this man die, his Lord will destroy us all."

When Peter appeared he calmed the people and said: "You people are soldiers of Christ and have all your hope in Christ! Remember the signs and wonders which you have seen through me. Remember the compassion and mercy of God and how many cures he has brought to you. Be patient and wait on Him, for when He comes, He shall reward every man according to his doings. And for now, hold no grievance against Agrippa, for he is the minister of his father's working - the evil one. But no matter what the evil one desires, all events come to pass as the Lord desires."

And Peter having approached and standing by the cross began to say: "O' name of the cross, your hidden mystery! Your name is too sacred to be uttered by human lips, the spirit part of man that cannot be separated from God. Love unspeakable and inseparable, I come to You now.

"Now that my race is over, I will explain your mystery. Never look upon this cross for hope in Christ, for nothing in this visual world represents Christ. The key is to separate your souls from everything that is of the physical senses, from everything that appears to the eyes, ears and touch. These senses only deceive you and distract you from the real truth, casting them into error. What you see, touch and hear is not real. Blind your eyes, close your ears, put away your doings that are seen of men and you shall perceive all that which concerns Christ. Only then will you learn the whole mystery of your salvation. It was probably a waste of words I just spoke because you still will not comprehend and understand. So now it is time for me, Peter, to deliver up this flawed body of this visual world unto them who take it. Receive it then, you evil prince of this world, unto whom it belongs. My only request is to crucify me with my head down."

When they hung Peter up in the manner he requested, he spoke again: "Listen carefully and learn the mystery of all nature. In the beginning the first man was born head downwards, as I appear hanging here. Since then, all has been turned upside down. Things of the right hand went to the left hand and things of the left, to the right. Man disturbed the entire order of nature. He made things unfair to be fair, evil to be good and a lie to be truth. The Lord told us: 'Unless you make the things of the right hand as those of the left and those of the left as those of the right and those that are above as those below and those that are behind as those that are before, you will not have knowledge of the kingdom.'

"The figure you now see hanging is the representation of the birth of the first man, who was born upside down. To make things right, you must cease from error and turn right side up. It is your salvation to hang upon the cross of Christ, who is the Word stretched out, the One and only. For what else is Christ, but the Word, the sound of God; so that the Word is the upright beam and the sound is the cross beam, the nature of man. And the nail which binds the beam to the upright is the conversion and repentance of man.

"This cross is thus called the tree of life. Lord, I give You thanks, not with this mouth and tongue that truth and falsehood spew forth, nor with this word whose only nature is material, but with a voice that is only perceived and understood in silence and not heard by ears, a corruptible substance. The silent voice I speak is not of this earth, or written in books, which are privy to one and not to another. But with this, O' Jesus Christ do I give thanks, with the silence of a voice, wherewith the spirit that is in me loves You, who can only be known by man's spirit. You are my father, my mother, my brother, my friend, my bondsman, my steward, my Lord and King. There is none other than You who can save my soul and life.

"Believers, run to Him in whom all truth exists. You will obtain those things good that He promised: 'which neither eye hath seen nor ear heard, neither have they entered into the heart of man.' We praise You, we give You thanks and confess to You, glorifying our Savior. Even we men who are without strength, for You are God alone and none other, to whom be glory now and unto all ages. Amen."

"what eye has not seen, and ear has not heard, and has not entered into the heart of man, what God has prepared for them that love Him. For God has revealed it to us by the Spirit. For the Spirit searches all things, even the deep things of God."

When all that stood by pronounced the Amen, Peter gave up his spirit unto the Lord.

Marcellus, a wealthy man, then took Peter down from the cross with his own hands and washed him in milk and wine, then prepared his body and placed it in a very expensive marble coffin and laid the coffin in its own dedicated tomb.

That night, Peter appeared to Marcellus and said: "Marcellus, have you heard that the Lord said: 'Let the dead be buried of their own dead?'"

Marcellus answered: "Yes."

Peter said: "The money you just spent on the dead is wasted. You being alive have acted like a dead man caring for the dead." And Marcellus awoke and told the other believers of Peter's appearance and Marcellus stayed with them until the coming of Paul unto Rome.

But Nero, learning that Peter had departed out of this life, was furious with Agrippa. Nero had big plans to kill Peter himself with greater torment, because Peter had caused many of those who served him to leave the emperor's service. For a long time Nero refused to talk to Agrippa and set out to destroy all of them that had been made disciples by Peter, but Nero had a dream where he was scourged and a voice said: "You cannot now persecute nor destroy the servants of Christ. Therefore remove your hands from them." And so Nero, frightened by such a vision, abstained from harming the disciples, but only for a time.

"Upon you, Peter, I will build My church; and the gates of Hades will not overpower it. I will give you the keys of the kingdom of heaven; and whatever you bind on earth shall have been bound in heaven, and whatever you loose on earth shall have been loosed in heaven."

"Glory be to God, the Father of our Lord and Savior with the Holy Ghost, world without end. Amen".

The rest of the life of Clement

Before Peter left for the cross, he ordained Clement to take over his position as head bishop, running the government of the Church of Rome.

(The Epistle of Clement to James - edited)

From Clement to James, brother of our lord, and the bishop of bishops, who rules Jerusalem, the holy church of the Hebrews.

Simon Peter was set apart to be the foundation of the Church by Jesus Himself. Peter, the first-fruits of our Lord, was the first of the apostles to whom the Father first revealed the Son; the excellent and approved disciple who was commanded to enlighten the darker part of this evil world and was enabled to accomplish it. Peter himself, by reason of his immense love towards men, clearly and publicly testified in opposition to the wicked one who failed to withstand him. There is to be a good King over all of the world.

Before Peter exchanged this existence for his eternal life, he suddenly seized my hand and rose up and said in presence of the church:

"I am done, my work is through, it is finished and I am excited. Since I, the apostle of the Lord and Teacher Jesus Christ am approaching the end of my work in this present temporary kingdom, I lay hands upon this Clement as your bishop. To him I entrust my chair of teaching, he who has journeyed with me from the beginning to the end and has heard and documented all my homilies. Having had a share in all my trials, he has been found steadfast in the faith, above all others - pious, philanthropic, pure, learned, chaste, good, upright and large-hearted.

"I have communicated to him the power of binding and loosing, so that everything which he shall ordain in the earth shall be done in the heavens. For he will bind what should be bound and loose what should be loosed, as knowing the role of the Church. Therefore listen to him and do as he says.

"O' Clement, with the time you are given, do battle on the side of our good King, Who is to give great rewards after victory. You have learned from me the administration of the Church for the safety of the brethren who are dependent on us.

"Shake off all the cares of life; do not be involved in any other secular business. For Christ does not wish to appoint you either a judge or an arbitrator in business, or negotiator of the secular affairs of the present life. Your service, by the word of truth, is to separate the good among men from the bad. Let the disciples do the administrative work and free you to be able to save.

"Let the Presbyters join the young in marriage, anticipating the dangers of youthful lusts. Let them not neglect the marriage of those who are older, for lust is vigorous even in some old men.

"Fornication and adultery are very terrible things. They hold second place in respect of punishment, the first being those who live in error, even though they be chaste.

"Above all things be careful about chastity, for fornication has been marked out as a bitter thing in the estimation of God. Adultery is that a man should not enjoy his own wife alone, or a woman should not enjoy her own husband alone. If anyone be chaste, he is able also to be philanthropic, on account of which he shall obtain eternal mercy. For as adultery is a great evil, so philanthropy is the greatest good.

"Love all your people with grave and compassionate eyes, performing to orphans the part of parents, to widows that of husbands, affording them sustenance with all kindliness, arranging marriages for those who are in their prime and for those who are without a profession, the means of necessary support through employment, giving work to the artificer and alms to the incapable. Feed the hungry, give drink to the thirsty and clothing to the naked; visit the sick; showing yourselves to those who are in prison, help them.

"For, the whole business of the Church is like unto a great ship, bearing through a violent storm with men who are of many places - a ship destined for the city of the good kingdom. God is our shipmaster, Christ our pilot, the bishop is the Pilot's mate. The sailors are deacons, midshipmen the catechists, the multitude of the saved people are the passengers. The world is the treacherous sea. Foul winds are temptations, persecutions, and all manner of afflictions to the waves. The land winds and their squalls are the discourses of deceivers and false prophets. Rugged rocks are the judges in high places threatening terrible things. The meetings of two seas and the wild places, are unreasonable men and those who doubt of the promises of truth.

"Regard hypocrites as pirates. Strong whirlpools, murderous wrecks and flounderings regard as sins. In order to sail with a fair wind, **pray so as to be heard, remembering that prayers are heard by doing good deeds**.

"What use is it, my brethren, if someone says he has faith but he has no works? ... Even so faith, if it has no works, is dead,...even demons believe in Christ....But are you willing to recognize, you foolish fellow, that faith without works is useless? ....You see that a man is justified by works and not by faith alone. ...For just as the body without the spirit is dead, so also faith without works is dead (James 2:14)".

"Let all pray to God for a prosperous voyage. Yet, let those sailing expect every tribulation, as traveling over a great and torturous sea."

Having thus spoken, Peter removed his pallium - the scarf he has worn through all our trials and travels. Peter laid his hands upon me in the presence of all, and compelled me to sit in his own chair and when I was seated, he said to me: "O' Clement, my work is now done; I have finished the race and am moving on to my lifelong dream - a paradise so wonderful, it is way beyond man's ability to comprehend. This pallium has served me well, but is no longer necessary where I am now going. I bestow upon you this pallium, my only worldly possession. It has become our battle flag, carrying us forward through the evil kingdom in triumph.

"James the brother of the Lord will get the greatest comfort knowing you are taking command of the chair of the teacher, after me. Amen."

"Our fight is not against people on earth but against the rulers and authorities and the powers of this world's darkness, against the spiritual powers of evil in the heavenly world." (Ephesians 6)

Comments

Some have considered Clement apostolic, a direct follower of Christ Himself because Clement spent so much of his life with the apostles Peter, Paul, Luke and Timothy and helped in their journeys' work and dangers. Just as Paul did not know Christ while He was on earth in human form, or was taught by Him for one to three years, yet everyone considers Paul an apostle.

Even though there were several bishops of Rome before Clement, I would still consider Clement the actual second Pope in command over all bishops and churches, after Peter.

The persecution came and went through Clement's years. Story has it that he was condemned of some crime and sent to the marble quarries on Pontus. He found many Christians there, where they had a freshwater problem; the only good drinking water was six miles away. So, the story has it that one day Clement saw a lamb pawing the ground. Clement took it as a sign and started digging at the spot the lamb was pawing and discovered a fresh water spring.

Even while imprisoned, Clement continued to convert many pagans. There is a legend that the authorities condemned him to be thrown into the sea, (allegation uncertain) with an anchor around his neck; thus the pictures of St Clement with an anchor at his side. His body was recovered by his disciple Phoebus and later (860 AD) transferred to Constantinople. Later again, it was transferred back to Rome where it is today, residing in the church of San Clemente.

The problem with all the legends is that none of the early church fathers writings mention such martyrdom. Certainly Clements martyrdom would be worth documenting.

Either way, Clement was a martyr, because he was wealthy and could easily have enjoyed the temporary impious pleasures of this life, but instead, sacrificed it all to labor for our Lord, Savior and King.

"We must consider all the things of this world as none of ours, and not desire to have them. This world and the new world to come are big enemies of each other. We, therefore, cannot, be friends to both. So, every person must decide which world to forsake, and which world he would enjoy being a subject of. We think, that it is better to hate the present things, as insufficient, very short-lived, and corruptible, and to love those which are to come, which are truly good and incorruptible. Let us prepare with all seriousness, for the combat we will face in this temporary world. Let us run in the straight road, the race that is incorruptible. This is what Christ said: '(Keep My commandments) keep your bodies pure and your souls without spot, that you may receive eternal life.' (The "Second Epistle" of St. Clement) "*

Clement, Son of Faustinianus, Bishop of Rome

Reference

Demons are in the food

When I first read the Recognitions, I was intrigued and humored. Angels mated with human women? I never noticed it before, but there it was, in Genesis 6 and Enoch. In another statement Peter explains something I have never heard in my life: "There are unclean spirits in the meat we eat." Once inside a person, unclean spirits can enlighten the mind to hidden knowledge and also influence the mind to fulfill their personal desires which are contrary to God's will. Peter says these demons inspired, in man's mind, the knowledge for all our technology, knowledge man could have never known without help. Yet, after cross referencing the statement with the Bible, it has been there all the time. Adam and Eve "ate" the forbidden fruit, the unclean fruit and the devil was now inside of them talking to their mind. "The day you eat from it your eyes will be opened and you will be like God, knowing good and evil..... the eyes of both of them were opened and they knew that they were naked." Before, their minds never comprehended such and God said, "Who told you that you were naked? (the devil now inside from the 'unclean' food) Have you eaten from the (unclean) tree of which I commanded you not to eat?....man might stretch out his hand, and take also from the tree of life, (the body and blood of Christ) and eat, and live forever therefore the Lord God sent Adam and Eve out from the garden of Eden." I could never understand what the difference was between a clean and an unclean animal until Peter explained it. I have heard all kinds of explanations, none of which made any sense, but after Peter says demons enter the body through the food and particularly the meat we eat, then unclean meat would mean food high in unclean spirits. Adam, Noah, John the Baptist and Peter were vegetarians. Why didn't Christ, for Passover supper, say "Eat this lamb (meat instead of bread), My body and drink this wine, My blood?" God and Moses tried to break the people of eating meat by giving them manna: "The rabble who were among them had greedy desires..... 'Who will give us meat to eat? ......There is nothing at all to look at except this manna.' .....the anger of the Lord was kindled greatly, and Moses was displeased...... 'O' that someone would give us meat to eat!......' Therefore the Lord will give you meat and you shall eat. (God is mad) You shall eat, not one day, nor two days, nor five days, nor ten days, nor twenty days, but a whole month, until it comes out of your nostrils and becomes loathsome to you; because you have rejected the Lord who is among you." (Numbers 11:10)

Not only did the demons or Nephilim start man killing and eating God's pets, man offered God some to eat also (sacrificing animals to God). Therefore man's practice of killing and eating animals became known as "eating at the table of demons", "meat sacrificed to idols" since eating animals was not of God but brought to us by the fallen angels. Killing an animal is sacrificing an animal for the eating pleasure of demons in your body, fulfilling their will in contrast to the will of God.

"So God created man in his own image, in the image of God created he him; male and female created he them. And God blessed them, and God said unto them, Be fruitful, and multiply, and replenish the earth, and subdue it: and have dominion over the fish of the sea, and over the fowl of the air, and over every living thing that moveth upon the earth. And God said, Behold, I have given you every herb bearing seed, which is upon the face of all the earth, and **every tree, in the which is the fruit of a tree yielding seed; to you it shall be for meat**. And to every beast of the earth, and to every fowl of the air, and to everything that creepeth upon the earth, wherein there is life, I have given every green herb for meat: and it was so. And God saw everything that he had made, and, behold, it was very good (until the 'watchers' came). (Genesis KJV)"

When Christ finally comes He says to "eat my body and drink my blood".(I am now inside of you to counter the unclean spirits from the meat you eat.) Unclean spirits will not cohabit with the Holy Spirit and visa-versa. After Clément's story of Peter was written, Christ tells Peter in a vision, it is now OK to eat meat with the gentiles. I am inside of you. You are protected. From the book of Acts: "I (Peter) also heard a voice saying to me, 'Get up, Peter; kill and eat.' But I said, 'By no means, Lord, for nothing unholy or unclean (demons) has ever entered my mouth'. But a voice from heaven answered a second time, 'What God has cleansed, by the body and blood of His Son, is no longer considered unholy'." It helps to explain "fasting". One would fast, not to deny himself, but to deny the demon's pleasure, showing who is in control of this body, you or they. Demons are mentioned eighty-two times in the Bible, the Devil thirty-two and Satan, fifty times. Christ and His apostles cast them out of people everywhere they went. Yet, demons are the elephant in the room. People today, even Christians, refuse to acknowledge them and consider people who talk about demons (the elephant) as "Kooks". Is something in a person's mind softly saying, "Ignore, ignore, demons (we) do not exist?"

Now we know why the demons asked Christ if they could go into the herd of pigs. Pigs are the preferred pleasure animal next to man; full of demons; the ultimate unclean animal as food. Pigs are high in intelligence and unrelenting in their quest for food, even becoming aggressive. They are sexually aggressive also, even the females.

The demons also knew the people would be eating the pigs allowing the demons back inside. So Christ sent the pigs over the cliff before the people could consume them.

Eucharist

God specifically prohibited the "drinking of blood" (Genesis 9:4, Deuteronomy 12:23, Leviticus 19:26). Eating of meat was forbidden before the "Watchers" came. Blood has the life and spirit in it and we are not allowed to consume it. The demons started this to satisfy their impious desire and man has continued their detestable practice. This is where our tales of vampires and werewolves comes from.

"Only you shall not eat the blood; you are to pour it out on the ground like water (Genesis, Deuteronomy, Leviticus, Acts)."

"...and the people ....took sheep and oxen and calves, and slew them on the ground; and the people ate them with the blood. Then they told Saul, saying, "Behold, the people are sinning against the Lord by eating with the blood." And he said, "You have acted treacherously (1 Samuel 14)."

Why would God now say: "OK people – now start drinking My blood."??
Why didn't our Lord say: "Eat this bread and drink this wine in remembrance of Me?" Instead of: "Eat My body and drink My blood?"

God's blood has the Holy Spirit, life in it. Animal/human blood has unclean spirits in it. "Contrary pairs", as Peter calls it, first the 'bad' then comes the 'good'.

Paul says eating meat is a demon sacrifice, but we no longer need to be concerned because of Christ's sacrifice. So eat at the table with the gentiles so as not to confuse the ones you are trying to give the message of salvation to. (1 Corinthians 10:16) Christ tells

Peter, "It is now permitted to eat meat." (Acts 11:5) Since Christ is now inside you from eating His body and drinking His blood, "often", He will repel and help (The Helper) you control the demons mind suggestions. Now you are free to eat anything you want. "He who eats My flesh and drinks My blood abides in Me, and I am inside of him" (John 6:56)

"Do often in remembrance of Me." "Remembrance" translated from Greek, can also be "bring Me to your memory" or "call Me to your mind." Now it makes sense – "Eat my body and drink My blood, often. Now I am inside you and can help you control your mind thoughts. I give you the mental strength to resist the demons."

Notice that Peter's Eucharist is his regular dinnertime or supper time as in "The Lord's Supper". As we would say a meal prayer, "Father we thank You for this food......" Peter might have said, "Father, thank You for the body and blood of Your Son, we are about to eat....bringing Your Holy Spirit inside our bodies....protecting us from evil and giving us the 'Helper' and everlasting life. Amen." Christ said "do often", so every suppertime would be "often". Paul also refers to the Eucharist as being a full regular meal (1 Corinthians 11:33).

Only the baptized believers were allowed to eat dinner with Peter. Demon possession is when you allow those demons in you to combine with your soul and take over control of your body instead of you controlling them. This is why "fasting" is important, - to drive out the demons. There is a warning given when partaking of the body and blood of Christ: If man's soul is intertwined with demons, it could do damage to the body. "Wherefore whosoever shall eat the bread or drink the cup of the

Lord in an unworthy manner,….. For he that eateth and drinketh, eateth and drinketh judgment unto himself, if he discern not the body. For this cause many among you are weak and sickly, and not a few sleep (died)."

"You cannot drink the cup of the Lord and the cup of demons; you cannot partake of the table of the Lord (His body) and the table of demons (animal body)" (1 Corinthians 10:21)

"how much more shall the blood of Christ, ….. **cleanse your conscience** (mind suggestions) from dead works to serve the living God?" (Hebrews 9:14) Cleanse you mind of the unclean spirits.

Old and New Covenant

Old Covenant - (Exodus 34:28) So he (Moses) was there with the Lord forty days and forty nights; he did not eat bread or drink water (Fasting, so the unclean spirits could not disturb his mind while he communicated with God). And he noted on the tablets the words of the covenant, the Ten Commandments.... (Exodus 24:12)

Now the Lord said to Moses: "Come up to Me on the mountain and remain there and I will give you the stone tablets with GOD's COMMANDMENTS which I have written for their instruction." So how will Moses make sure the people will follow God's commandments? Moses created "Moses law" or "The Law", which will force the people to keep the commandments, God's law. Leviticus lays down the law which explains how, by force, the covenant, Ten Commandments will be followed, or die.

So He declared to you His covenant which He commanded you to perform, by the force of Moses Law. Break a Commandment, and Moses (law) will kill you.

Most of the Old Testament shows examples in history of the blessings, when God's people kept the statutes and curses when the people did not obey. This would cycle over and over and Moses's law is obviously not going to work. The desire to keep the commandments needed to come from within, come from the heart, not by force from without. The demons persuasion inside were more powerful than the fear of punishment by man.

The New Covenant - After eating Christ's body for supper: "He took the cup also after supper, saying, 'This cup is the new covenant in My blood; do this, as often as you drink it, in remembrance of Me.'"

The KJ Bible interpretation

This cup is the NEW TESTAMENT in my BLOOD. Drink this often in REMEMBERANCE of Me.

For as long as you eat this bread and drink this cup you do SHOW the LORDS DEATH until he COME

Well, the Lord is not dead. He is alive and well in control, living inside anyone who desires.

Other definitions for the same Greek words

This cup is the COVENANT (for) my CHILDREN (KINDRED). Drink this often TO CALL (BRING) ME (IN)TO YOUR MIND. (for protection from demon suggestions to your mind).

For as long as you eat this bread and drink this cup you do PUT INTO ACTION the CONTROLING STRENGHT until I RETURN VISABLY.

In Luke, when Christ came back from the dead, He "broke bread" with two of the disciples. (After they consumed His body) They then recognized Him (Remembrance, Call to your Mind).

"He Who lives inside of you is greater than he who is in the world..... we live in Him and He lives inside of us: because He has given to us of His Holy Spirit."

This is why you fill your body with the Holy Spirit (Eucharist) and keep him there happy by reading the Word. So He can guard and protect you from the unseen enemy - the unwanted suggestions upon your mind.

With the demons out of control of one's body and Christ inside, one will desire to keep Gods commandments out of love. It will not require force from the outside. (John 6:56) "He who eats My flesh and drinks My blood abides in Me, and I in him." I (Christ) will now be inside man when he eats My body and drinks My blood. Man will now love my commandments, and force (The Law, Moses Law) will no longer be required for man to keep My commandments. My covenant will be written on their hearts. (Hebrews 8:10, 2 Corinthians 3)

The law is gone, BUT not the Commandments. "Whoever therefore breaks one of the least of these commandments, and teaches men so, shall be called least in the kingdom of heaven; but whoever does and teaches them, he shall be called great in the kingdom of heaven" (Matthew 5:19).

With the old covenant the commandments were kept by force. With the new covenant the commandments are kept by desire within one's heart - a love of God's will.

Today the "law" is no longer needed, that is the "law of Moses". The Ten Commandments are still in place. The law is done away with because we now have the new covenant to help us keep the commandments by our own "free will", our own choosing.

"Do not think that I came to abolish (God's) Law ....For truly I say to you, until heaven and earth pass away, not the smallest letter or stroke shall pass from (God's) Law until all is accomplished (Matthew 5:17)".

Heaven, Hades & Hell

This is the reason for the Gospel; The Good News; The salvation of souls.

If I am saved, what am I saved from?

The Rich Man and Lazarus: "Now there was a rich man, and he habitually dressed in purple and fine linen, joyously living in splendor every day. And a poor man named Lazarus was laid at his gate, covered with sores, and longing to be fed with the crumbs which were falling from the rich man's table; even the dogs were coming and licking his sores. Now the poor man died and was carried away by the angels to Abraham's bosom; and the rich man also died and was buried. In Hell he lifted up his eyes, being in torment, and saw Abraham far away and Lazarus in his bosom. And he cried out and said, 'Father Abraham, have mercy on me, and send Lazarus so that he may dip the tip of his finger in water and cool off my tongue, for I am in agony in this flame.' But Abraham said, 'Child, remember that during your life you received your good things, and likewise Lazarus bad things; but now he is being comforted here, and you are in agony. And besides all this, between us and you there is a great chasm fixed, so that those who wish to come over from here to you will not be able, and that none may cross over from there to us.' And he said, 'Then I beg you, father, that you send him to my father's house for I have five brothers in order that he may warn them, so that they will not also come to this place of torment.' But Abraham said, 'They have Moses and the Prophets; let them hear them.' But he said, 'No, father Abraham, but if someone goes to them from the dead, they will repent!' But he said to him, 'If they do not listen to Moses and the Prophets, they will not be persuaded even if someone rises from the dead'" (Luke 16:21).

"And the devil who had deceived them was thrown into the lake of fire and sulfur where the beast and the false prophet were, and they will be tormented day and night forever and ever" (Revelation 20:10).

Hades (Purgatory, Sleeping)

All the Old Testament kings are "sleeping" with their fathers.

"Listen, I tell you a mystery: We will not all sleep, (in the safe secure holding place for the dead souls, (Hades or Purgatory, who did not yet go straight to heaven) but we will all be changed in a flash, in the twinkling of an eye, at the last trumpet. For, the trumpet will sound, the dead will be raised imperishable, and we will be changed. Then the believers will be caught up into the clouds to meet Jesus and to escort him back to the earth." (1 Corinthians 15:52)

"Our friend Lazarus sleepeth; but I go, that I may awake him out of sleep. Then said his disciples, Lord, if he sleep, he shall do well.... Then said Jesus unto them plainly, Lazarus is dead." (John 11)

"Then I saw a great white throne and Him who sat upon it, from whose presence earth and heaven fled away, and no place was found for them. And I saw the dead, the great and the small, standing before the throne, and books were opened; and another book was opened, which is the 'book of life'; and the dead were judged from the things which were written in the books, according to their deeds (while in this present kingdom). And the sea gave up the dead that were in it, and death and Hades (Purgatory) gave up the dead that were (sleeping) in them; and they were judged, every one of them according to the deeds they did when alive on earth. Then death and Hades were thrown into the lake of fire (The places were no longer needed). This is the second death, the lake of fire. And if anyone's name was not in the book of life....." (Revelation 20:11)

He stores up the things in Hades, the holding-place the Catholics call Purgatory, designating it as the place of souls. "Christ visited and made a proclamation to the spirits, now in prison, who were once disobedient" (1 Peter 3:19). "And why do you not even on your own initiative judge what is right? ..... I say to you, you will not get out of there (Hades) until you have paid the very last cent. (debt)" (Luke 12:57) "I will penetrate to all the lower parts of the earth, and will behold all that sleep, and will enlighten all that hope in the Lord (Ecclesiasticus)."

There is another historical writing that was found in fragments called The Apocalypse of Peter. It was also documented by Clement and explains heaven and hell. Like the Revelation of John, Christ takes Peter to Heaven and to Hell. This writing was a popular early Christian text of the 2nd century that some churches included along with the New Testament Scriptures. So, there could very well be some authenticity.

The Apocalypse of Peter, also documented by Clement - edited

"While He was with us on earth my Lord took me to the 'day of judgment': what will come upon man in the last days, the "day of judgment", when the present world will be no more. All the children of men will be gathered together before our Creator who lives forever. And he shall command the earth to release all those bodies that have dissolved and all will be restored and reappear as they existed before, in the same bodies they lived in during this present kingdom, for nothing has ever perished before God, and nothing is impossible with Him, because all things are His.

"And soul and spirit will be given the old bodies at the command of God, thus will complete the rising of the dead, for the 'day of judgment'. Raised up in that day will be those who believed in Him and are chosen of Him and those who did not believe - all the people for whom He made the world in the first place. God will separate those who will go on to the new eternal kingdom from those who will be destroyed in eternal Hell. On that day, not only will the visible world be judged, but heaven also (the fallen angels).

"For the unbelievers, those who fell away from faith in God and who have committed sin, floods of fire shall be let loose; and darkness and obscurity shall come up and clothe and veil the whole world and the waters shall be changed and turned into coals of fire and all that is in them shall burn, and the sea shall become fire. Under the heaven shall be a sharp fire that cannot be quenched and flows to fulfill the judgment of wrath. And the stars shall fly into pieces by flames of fire, as if they had not even been created and the powers of the heaven shall pass away for lack of water and shall be as though they had never been. The whole earth will be a boiling mass of fire.

"Then all will see Christ coming upon an eternal cloud of brightness, and the angels of God that are with Him shall sit upon the throne of His glory at the right hand of His Heavenly Father. Then God will set a crown upon His Sons head, and all people will be emotionally moved at the sight.

"Then the works of all people will be placed before Him, to every man according to his deeds as he lived in the first world. As for the elect who believed in Him and **did 'good' according to His commandments**, will come unto Him and not see death by the devouring fire of the earth. But the unrighteous, the sinners and the hypocrites shall stand in the depths of darkness that shall not pass away, and their chastisement is the fire. The angels will bring forward their sins and prepare for them a place wherein they shall be punished for ever, every one according to his transgression.

"And even those (the Watchers, Titans) whom men called gods, will burn with them in everlasting fire. After that all of them with their dwelling places will be destroyed, and shall be punished eternally.

"Then all who lived and were not in the "book of life" will be condemned to the place prepared for them. Those who blasphemed will be hung by their tongues over an unquenchable fire, never to escape, and never to be free of that torment.

"In another place is a pit, great and full. In it are those who have denied righteousness, and angels of punishment chastise and torment them with fire.

"I saw other women of error hanging by their neck, and by their hair. Others, men and women, were being herded up a mountain and thrown off a cliff, then collected at the bottom and herded back up, repeating over and over and over with no rest from this punishment.

(You get the picture. It explains each punishment for each sin. From here it gets really gross, being eaten by worms and such, so I will skip over.)

"....... thereafter the angels will bring His elect and righteous and cloth them and tend to them. They will gaze upon those in torment, especially those being tormented who were evil to His elect while they were alive on earth.

"Now being too late, those who are in torment will scream for mercy. For now they realize the judgment of God, which he declared before, and they mocked and laughed and refused to believe. Then the angel of Tartarus (Hell) will come and torment them further and ask: 'So now do you repent, when it is no longer the time for repentance and all your opportunities are long gone?' And they will agree that their punishment is just and good, for we all are receiving according to our deeds.

"Then He will adorn His elect with gifts and lead them away rejoicing, and they will enter His everlasting kingdom. Only then will they be able to grasp a paradise beyond simple man's comprehension. The Father has committed all judgments to His Son, the destiny of sinners and their eternal doom." Then I, Peter said: " My Lord, this is unbearable" and I begged my Lord to have pity on them.

Believers can rescue unbelievers in Hell, at their option.

Christ replied: "The only reason I came was for those who believed in me. So for the same who have believed in me, if they ask, I will have pity on whomever they would like. If they choose, I will grant them the grace to pardon any unbeliever they would like and pull out of eternal tormenting hell a friend, loved one or child who was too stubborn to listen or believe as there will be no sadness in My new Kingdom. Peter, you are allowed to understand this but keep this part to yourself. Sinners will not understand and will sin even more if they learn a righteous friend or relative will bail them out.

(After Judgment)"This earth will be rolled up like a scroll and a new earth created, like a chick breaking out of his egg and emerging anew. The eggshell must be destroyed in order for a more wonderful creation to emerge and grow.

"Now that I have shown this to you Peter, who was chosen according to the promise which I have given you, go and spread my gospel throughout the world. The chosen shall rejoice and my words shall be the source of hope and of life."

Then my Lord Jesus Christ our King said: "Let us go unto the holy mountain." I and the other disciples went with him, praying. When we arrived there were two men we could not look at because a light shone from their faces stronger than the sun and their clothing shone like nothing I can compare to in this world. Their appearance was astonishing and wonderful. On their heads were crowns woven of flowers and their hair was like rainbows. I asked my Lord who they were, and He replied: "Moses and Elijah." I asked: "Are Abraham, Isaac and Jacob here also?" And He showed us a great garden that had the odor of perfume, the abode of all who were persecuted for His sake. I asked: "Will you let me make three houses of worship, one for You, and one for Moses, and one for Elijah?" And my Lord replied disturbed: "Satan's war on you has blocked your understanding of the good things of this unseen world. Our places are not fashioned with human hands but by our Father" and we beheld and were amazed. Then came a great white cloud over our heads and took away our Lord, Moses and Elijah. I trembled and was afraid, and we looked up and the heaven opened and men like us greeted our

Lord and accompanied them to another heaven. Then the heaven closed shut.

Peter said to me, Clement: "God created all things for his glory. The Son at his coming will raise the dead and will make His righteous ones shine seven times more than the sun and will make their crowns shine like crystal and like the rainbow in the time of rain; they will be perfumed; their beauty and appearance cannot be expressed." Being there with James and John the sons of Zebedee, the bright cloud overshadowed us and we heard the voice of the Father saying unto us: "This is my Son whom I love and in whom I am well pleased." We forgot all the things of this life and we talked in garble because of the greatness of the wonder of that day and the showing to us of the second coming and the kingdom for ever and ever.

Interesting for animal lovers; Animal souls will be at judgment to witness for or against you. "And as every soul of man is judged, similarly the souls of beasts which the Lord created, will accuse man, if he feed them ill" (Book of the secrets of Enoch).

"I went in (to Heaven) and approached a wall which is built of crystals and surrounded by tongues of fire, and I went into the tongues of fire and drew close to a large house which was built of crystals. The walls of the house were like mosaic crystals, and its floor was of crystal. Its ceiling was like the path of the stars and between them were fiery cherubim, and their heaven was clear as water. A flaming fire surrounded the walls, and its doors and windows blazed with fire. I entered into that house, and it was hot as fire and cold as ice. And behold! there was a second house, greater than this one, and the entire door stood open before me, and it was built of flames of fire. And in every respect it so excelled in splendor and magnificence and extent that there are no man made words to describe it. I looked and saw inside a lofty throne: its appearance was as crystal, and the wheels thereof as the shining sun And there were cherubim. Seraphin, Cherubic, and Ophannin: who sleep not And guard the throne of His glory. And I saw so many angels they could not be counted, A thousand thousands, and ten thousand times ten thousand, encircling that house. Michael, and Raphael, and Gabriel, and Phanuel, and the holy angels who are above the heavens, go in and out of that house. And with them the Head of Days, His head white and pure as wool, And His raiment indescribable. And from underneath the throne came streams of flaming fire so that I could not look thereon. The Great Glory sat upon the throne, and His clothing shone more brightly than the sun and was whiter than any snow. None of the angels could enter and behold His face by reason of the magnificence and glory and no flesh could behold Him.

Then the Lord called me and said: 'Come here, Enoch, and hear my word.' I approach the door: and I bowed my face downwards" (Book of Enoch).

Ten Commandments

The Ten Words, Decalogue, Ten Commandments.

This is what it's all about!!

These are rules of God for one's own protection from demons and to allow us to be good enough to have a relationship with God, and make it to the new kingdom.

Man was aware of them before Moses, but his written account is our first concise documentation.

Rule number one, the first four commandments, our relationship with our Creator.

'Love the Lord your God with all your heart and with all your soul and with all your mind.'

1) Do not have any other gods except me,

A feeling of profound love and admiration for God alone and nothing else. God will rule every aspect of your life if you let Him. Do not depend on governments, presidents, kings, money, lucky charms, astrology, man or any created thing. Thank Him for everything that happens to you regardless of your opinion - of your situation.

2) Do not make for yourself any graven image, or any likeness of anything that is in heaven above or that is in the earth beneath or that is in the water under the earth;

This is probably the most sensitive of all the commandments. Man has never seen God, but man just is not satisfied unless he erects some form, "image", a visual representative of God to gaze upon, buildings, statues or paintings.

Give honor to the image of God, which is man. Give food to the hungry, drink to the thirsty, clothing to the naked, hospitality to the stranger, and necessary things to the prisoner. That is what will be regarded as true worship bestowed upon God. All these things we do for our fellow man go to the honor of God's image and build up treasures in the kingdom to come.

"Without works, there is no faith."

3) Do not use the Lord's name in vain - empty, futile, worthless, hollow, common, as with all other words.

Use the Lords name in praise and thanksgiving ONLY, glorifying the Great Creator. "Hallowed be Thy Name." God, Christ and the Holy Ghost are worthy only of glory. "You can use the other 1,013,910 words any way your heart desires;"

4) Remember the Sabbath day to keep it holy.
Work six days a week, rest your animals and people on the seventh day just as God rested His creation. Rest your land on the seventh year.

Rule number two: 'Love your neighbor as yourself.' - is the next six Commandments, the image of God – "good works". What you do to your fellow man is done to God and will be returned to you in like kind; mercy, forgiveness, prosperity – "forgive us our debts as we forgive others".

5) Honor your father and your mother

6) Do not kill. Do not shed "innocent blood", which is different from defending yourself in war or imposing the death sentence. Someone who has shed innocent blood is deserving of death. A Good Shepherd will protect his sheep from enemy attack or a murderer - wolves, bears and lions. If he really loves his sheep, a good shepherd will never allow a wolf back into the sheep.

7) Do not commit adultery.

8) Do not steal.

9) Do not give false evidence against your neighbor. This is different from telling a lie - it is a lie that damages another person, as a witness who lies, causing an innocent person to endure unjust punishment at the hands of man.

10) Do not covet your neighbor's possessions: his house, his wife, his manservant, or his maidservant, his ox, his ass, or anything that is your neighbor's, lusting for what is not yours.

"Well said Teacher," the man replied. "You are right in saying that God is one and there is no other but Him. To love Him with all your heart, with all your understanding and with all your strength, and to love your neighbor as yourself is more important than all burnt offerings and sacrifices" (Mark 12:33).

"Do not think that I came to abolish the Law or the Prophets; I did not come to abolish but to fulfill. For truly I say to you, until heaven and earth pass away, not the smallest letter or stroke shall pass from the Law (The commandments, God's Law which is different from Moses' law) until all is accomplished. Whoever then annuls one of the least of these commandments, and teaches others to do the same, shall be called least in the kingdom of heaven; but whoever keeps and teaches them, he shall be called great in the kingdom of heaven" (Matthew 5:17).

That is it!

Only Ten Rules! How simple!

Notice what is missing?

"The commandments of man":

Gluttony, drinking alcohol, tobacco use and many more. These are undesirable human habits BUT they are not sins.

God gave only Ten Rules and the breaking of any of the Ten Commandments is a sin, an error, resulting in suffering (correction). It does not include the other 100+ commandments of men; all the stuff man has added.

"Listen very carefully and comprehend: It is not what goes into the mouth of a man that makes him unclean and defiled, but it is what comes out of the mouth that defiles man....whatever comes out of the mouth comes from the heart, and this is what makes a man unclean and defiles ...Do you not understand that whatever goes into the mouth passes through the body and back to the earth... but out of the heart come evil thoughts such as murder, adultery, sexual vice, theft, false witnessing, slander, and irreverent speech." (Matthew 15)

"...unclean demons, which had taken possession of very many, were expelled by the Savior from the bodies of the sufferers, who are said also to be made free by Him" (Origen – Third century AD).

"By guarding against sinning, we guard against suffering" (Clement of Alexandria – Second century AD).

"For if we go on sinning willfully after receiving the knowledge of the truth, there no longer remains a sacrifice for sins, [27] but a terrifying expectation of judgment...." (John 17).

The Creed – "I believe"

They were having problems with people like Simon changing the true Gospel so they created a declaration of the true faith – a profession of the true faith. The Apostles' Creed was composed around the 2nd century and the Nicene Creed in 325 AD amended it to clarify: "Christ was 'begotten' of God His Father and not 'created' by God.

"We believe in one God,
the Father, the Almighty,
maker of heaven and earth,
of all that is, seen and unseen.

We believe in one Lord, Jesus Christ,
the only Son of God,
eternally begotten of the Father, (not created but was with the Father from the beginning.)
God from God, light from light,
true God from true God,
begotten, not made,
of one Being with the Father;
through him all things were made.
For us and for our salvation (from eternal destruction)
he came down from heaven,
was incarnate of the Holy Spirit and the Virgin Mary
and became truly human.
For our sake he was crucified under Pontius Pilate;
he suffered death and was buried.
On the third day he rose again
in accordance with the Scriptures;
he ascended into heaven
and is seated at the right hand of the Father.

He will come again in glory to judge the living and the dead
(Judgment Day),
and his (New) kingdom will have no end.

We believe in the Holy Spirit, the giver of life,
who proceeds from the Father [and the Son],
who with the Father and the Son is worshiped and glorified,
who has spoken through the prophets.
We believe in one holy catholic (Universal) and apostolic
(Original) Church (All the people who believe this Creed).
We acknowledge one baptism for the forgiveness of sins.
We look for the resurrection of the dead (When Christ returns),
and the life of the world to come (Kingdom of our Christ, the
Good Prince) fore ever and ever. Amen."

Example of my Paraphrase for friends and family of the 1884 Translation Ante-Nicene Fathers

Below is from the Recognitions Book III:

Chapter XVII.-Not Admitted by All.

Then Simon, interrupting his discourse, said: "They do rightly who say that there is no evil." Then Peter answered: "We do not propose to speak of this now, but only to state the fact that the existence of evil is not universally admitted. But the second question that you should have asked is, What is evil?-a substance, an accident, or an act? And many other things of the same sort. And after that, towards what, or how it is, or to whom it is evil,-whether to God, or to angels, or to men, to the righteous or the wicked, to all or to some, to one's self or to no one? And then you should inquire, Whence it is?-whether from God, or from nothing; whether it has always been, or has had its beginning in time; whether it is useful or useless? and many other things which a proposition of this sort demands." To this Simon answered: "Pardon me; I was in error concerning the first question; but suppose that I now ask first, whether evil is or not? "

Chapter XXIII. Origin of Evil.

Then said Peter: "I shall speak, not as under compulsion from you, but at the request of the hearers. The power of choice is the sense of the soul, possessing a quality by which it can be inclined towards what acts it wills." Then Simon, applauding Peter for what he had spoken, said: "Truly you have expounded it magnificently and incomparably, for it is my duty to bear testimony to your speaking well. Now if you will explain to me this which I now ask you, in all things else I shall submit to you. What I wish to learn, then, is this: if what God wishes to be, is; and what He does not wish to be, is not. Answer me this." Then Peter: "If you do not know that you are asking an absurd and incompetent question, I shall pardon you and explain; but if you are aware that you are asking inconsequently, you do not well." Then Simon said: "I swear by the Supreme Divinity, whatsoever that may be, which judges and punishes those who sin, that I know not what I have said inconsequently, or what absurdity there is in my words, that is, in those that I have just uttered."

Chapter XXIV.-God the Author of Good, Not of Evil.

To this Peter answered: "Since, then, you confess that you are ignorant, now learn. Your question demanded our deliverance on two matters that are contrary to one another. For every motion is divided into two parts, so that a certain part is moved by necessity, and another by will; and those things which are moved by necessity are always in motion, those which are moved by will, not always. For example, the sun's motion is performed by necessity to complete its appointed circuit, and every state and service of heaven depends upon necessary motions. But man directs the voluntary motions of his own actions. And thus there are some things which have been created for this end, that in their services they should he subject to necessity, and should be unable to do aught else than what has been assigned to them; and when they have accomplished this service, the Creator of all things. who thus arranged them according to His will, preserves them. But there are other things, in which there is a power of will, and which have a free choice of doing what they will. These, as I have said, do not remain always in that order in which they were created: but according as their will leads them, and the judgment of their mind inclines them, they effect either good or evil; and therefore He hath proposed rewards to those who do well, and penalties to those who do evil.(10)

Chapter XXV.-"Who Hath Resisted His Will? "

You say, therefore, if God wishes anything to be, it is; and if He do not wish it, it is not. But if I were to answer that what He wishes is, and what He wishes not is not, you would say that then He wishes the evil things to be which are done in the world, since everything that He wishes is, and everything that He wishes not is not. But if I had answered that it is not so that what God wishes is, and what He wishes not is not, then you would retort upon me that God must then be powerless, if He cannot do what He wills; and you would be all the more petulant, as thinking that you had got a victory, though had said nothing to the point. Therefore you are ignorant, O Simon, yea very ignorant, how the will of God acts in each individual case. For some things, as we have said, He has so willed to be, that they cannot be otherwise than as they are ordained by Him; and to these He has assigned neither rewards nor punishments; but those which He has willed to be so that they have it in their power to do what they will, He has assigned to them according to their actions and their wills, to earn either rewards or punishments. Since, therefore, as I have informed you, all things that are moved are divided into two parts, according to the distinction that I formerly stated, everything that God wills is, and everything that He wills not is not.

Chapter LIX.-Good and Evil in Pairs.

"For, as I was beginning to say,(33) God has appointed for this world certain pairs; and he who comes first of the pairs is of evil, he who comes second, of good. And in this is given to every man an occasion of right judgment, whether he is simple or prudent. For if he is simple, and believes him who comes first, though moved thereto by signs and prodigies, he must of necessity, for the same reason, believe him who comes second; for he will be persuaded by signs and prodigies, as he was before. When he believes this second one, he will learn from him that he ought not to believe the first, who comes of evil; and so the error of the former is corrected by the emendation of the latter. But if he will not receive

STOP

Below is my interpretation of the above. My paraphrase actually includes more discussions on this subject than just the sample above. It has both Clementine Recognitions and also the Homilies and parts from the KJ Bible inserted where relevant.

From my composition, page 62.

(Simon) Since your God, as you say, made all things, why did He create evil?"

Peter responded: "The existence of evil is not known or admitted by everyone because only the true Prophet knows of it. Every motion is divided into two parts, one part is moved by necessity, and the other by will. Those by necessity are always in constant predictable motion. But those which are moved by their 'will' can vary. For example, the sun's motion is fixed and predictable and every state and service of heaven depends upon fixed motions. The sun, moon, and earth, are in a fixed unchangeable motion through time and space. But man can vary his state. He can choose or change his direction. Man directs the voluntary motions of his own actions. Thus the things of necessity are unable to do anything else. But men and angels have a power of will, which gives them free choice to do what they desire. Life is where their will leads them. It is where their hearts are, and the desires of their minds direct them. This 'free will' creates either 'good' or 'evil', depending on the direction one chooses. Good and evil are contrary pairs that define each other. 'Good' could not exist unless there was 'evil'. Therefore God has arranged rewards to those who do well, and penalties to those who do evil. Neither God nor the devil creates evil; man brings evil into existence by his own actions. Man's and angel's own 'free will' created evil."

Early references to the Recognitions

The earliest date: Clementines were twice quoted by Origen who lived from 184 to 253 AD

Eusebius the historian around 325 AD notes the Clement epistle to the church in Corinth was authentic; "accepted by all", but says the Recognitions seemed new to everyone. Yet if Origen spoke of them 100 years before Eusebius, Eusebius was just unaware.

"And certain men have lately brought forward other wordy and lengthy writings under his (Clements) name, containing dialogues of Peter and Apion."

This quote below was interesting because I noticed whoever wrote the Clement epistles has "similar character in regard to style and thoughts" as whoever wrote the Recognitions; "the epistle of Clement and that to the Hebrews have a similar character in regard to style, and still further because the thoughts contained in the two works are not very different." (The same author)

The Clementines are used by Ebionites around 360 AD .
St. Jerome references them in 387 and 392

So if someone, besides Clement, made up the Recognitions (fiction), who was that someone? Whoever might have written the Clementine Recognitions had inside information none of the other historic authors had. Where did they get such knowledge of the unseen world? And unlike the other writers, the writer of the Recognitions is not ambiguous. They state it bluntly and clearly to the point with much authority and accuracy.

We know of no other Clement of the first and second century's who would have the authority to address a homily to the Corinthian church.

Why would some other church father or theologian use the name "Clement" instead of his own?

This was a very interesting note on another old writing, "The Apocalypse of Peter", which also claims was documented by Clement.
"Peter orders Clement to hide this revelation in a box, that foolish men may not see it."

Peter has Clement document the Recognitions and send a copy to James in Jerusalem. Did Peter tell Clement to keep this hidden so "that foolish men may not see it", also? Was it just sent to James for his information and few if any copies ever made or survived?

RUFINUS - 340 – 410 AD was a monk, historian, and theologian. He was a translator of Greek documents into Latin.

A correspondence from Rufinus to Gaudentius (Bishop of Brescia from 387 until 410)

THE PREFACE TO THE BOOKS OF RECOGNITIONS OF ST. CLEMENT

Translated to English by Rev. William Henry Fremantle (early 1900's)

….my dear Gaudentius, …..this work is nothing but the payment of a debt due to the command laid upon me by the virgin Sylvia whose memory I revere. She it was who demanded of me, as you have now done by the right of heirship, to translate Clement into our language. The debt is paid at last, though after many delays. It is a part of the booty, and in my opinion no small one, which I have carried off from the libraries of the Greeks, and which I am collecting for the use and advantage of our countrymen. …I present to you Clement returning to Rome. I present him dressed in a Latin garb (translating Clements words from Greek to

Latin).…. It is but right that you, who have read this work in the Greek should point out to other's the design of my translation-- unless indeed, you feel that in some respects I have not observed the right method of rendering the original. You are, I believe well aware that there are two Greek editions of this work of Clement, his Recognitions; that there are two sets of books, which in some few cases differ from each other though the bulk of the narrative is the same. (The Reconitions do not exist today in Greek only Rufinus's translation to Latin) For instance, the last part of the work, that which gives an account of the transformation of Simon Magus, exists in one of these, while in the other it is entirely absent. On the other hand there are some things, such as the dissertation on the unbegotten and the begotten God, and a few others, which, though they are found in both editions, are, to say the least of them, beyond my understanding; and these I have preferred to leave others to deal with rather than to present them in an inadequate manner. As to the rest, I have taken pains not to swerve, even in the slightest degree from either the sense or the diction; and this, though it makes the expression less ornate, renders it more faithful.

There is a letter in which this same Clement writing to James the
Lord's brother, gives an account of the death of Peter…

(This would have to refer to "The Apocalypse of Peter" since Peters death is not in the Recognitions.)

and says that he has left him as his successor, as ruler and teacher of the church; and further incorporates a whole scheme of ecclesiastical government. This I have not prefixed to the work, both because it is later in point of time, and because it has been previously translated and published by me. ….Linus and Cletus were Bishops of the city of Rome before Clement. How then, some men ask, can Clement in his, letter to James say that Peter passed over to him his position as a church-teacher. Linus and Cletus were, no doubt,' Bishops in the city of Rome before

Clement, but this was in Peter's life-time; that is, they took charge of the episcopal work, while he discharged the duties of the apostolate. He is known to have done the same thing at Caesarea; for there, he had at his side Zacchaeus whom he had ordained as Bishop. Thus we may see how both things may be true; namely how they stand as predecessors of Clement in the list of Bishops, and yet how Clement after the death of Peter became his successor in the teacher's chair. But it is time that we should pay attention to the beginning of Clement's own narrative, which he addresses to James the Lord's brother.

The quote below from the "Second Epistle" of St. Clement is the identical message of the Clementine Homilies and Recognitions. Both authors are the same.

"This world and the next are two enemies. The one urges to adultery and corruption, avarice and deceit; the other bids farewell to these things. We cannot, therefore, be the friends of both; and it behooves us, by renouncing the one, to make sure of the other. Let us reckon that it is better to hate the things present, since they are trifling, and transient, and corruptible; and to love those [which are to come,] as being good and incorruptible. For if we do the will of Christ, we shall find rest; otherwise, nothing shall deliver us from eternal punishment, if we disobey His commandments."

"Yet one must realize humans are never allowed to see and understand, no matter how intelligent they think they are, until they first truly believe in Christ, the Son of God, Creator of the universe and our entire existence. God has put a supernatural block on the stubborn self-important unbelieving, but the humble believer, in the privacy of his heart, continues rejoicing and giving thanks for his newly found treasures and wisdom, delighting in the practice of good works and fantasizing about his future inheritance, the new world to come, when he will meet God, the King and Creator of all."

www.ingramcontent.com/pod-product-compliance
Lightning Source LLC
LaVergne TN
LVHW051459080426
835509LV00017B/1821